Rusty George • Jeff Krajewski

HERDING CATS

Teaching and Leading in a Postmodern World

COLLEGE PRESS PUBLISHING
JOPLIN, MISSOURI

Library of Congress Cataloging-in-Publication Data

George, Rusty, 1971–
    Herding cats: teaching and leading in a postmodern world /
Rusty George and Jeff Krajewski.
        p.   cm.
    Includes bibliographical references.
    ISBN 0-89900-873-9 (pbk.)
    1. Christian leadership.   I. Krajewski, Jeff, 1970–   .
II. Title.
BV652.1.G46 2001
253—dc21
                                                        2001047079

Herding Cats

Teaching and Leading in a Postmodern World

ACKNOWLEDGMENTS

Rich Mullins once said, "There is music you make, and there is music that makes you." We feel that this book is not something that we have written, but rather the stories and people that have made us. We truly are the ongoing artistry of the hand of our Designer and his people, and we want to thank not only him for his mercy, but also these foremost artists:

Rusty

Lorrie: Your encouragement and love have been the strength for my climb and the net for my fall. Thanks for letting us take this journey together. I love you. My family: You have taught me the beauty of discipline and dedication, and most importantly have shown me Jesus. Steve Meyers, Jeff Krajewski, Lance Peterson, Matt Harris, Landis Brown, John Presko, Rob McDowell, Jim Greenwood, Bret Foster, Jay McChord and Todd Elliot: Thank you for your faithfulness as we work together, though sometimes while apart. Monte Wilkinson (the ultimate young adult minister): Thanks for giving me a chance. Mike Breaux: Thanks for giving me your trust. The Young Adult Staff—T.D. Oakes, Charlotte Stephenson, Michelle Greenwood, and Brian Marshall: Thanks for ministering to me as well as with me. And finally, the Young Adult and 608 Ministries of Southland Christian Church: You have given me grace and direction as we've served together, and it's been an amazing blessing to work with you.

Jeff

Nicole: You have given me more of your love than I could have ever imagined possible. Thank you for standing beside me and for holding my hand. I love you. Tucker and Kezley: You are precious gifts from God and your Daddy loves you, thanks for loving me back. Mom, Dad, and Murph: Thank you for giving me a healthy and godly home through which I could learn to love Jesus. Rusty George: Thank you for your friendship. Ken Osness: Thank you for a willing ear to listen and your words of encouragement to follow my passion. Don Keehner: Thank you for sharing your wall and your life. You are a true friend. The members of Traders Point Christian Church: Thank you for giving me a place to grow up. Howard Brammer: Thank you for looking past the rough exterior of the young man I was and giving me a chance to make mistakes. Chris Croyts and Kenneth Sumner: Thank you for all that you have taught me and all that we will continue to learn as we minister together. And finally, to the Common Ground family: Thank you for providing my family with a loving and caring community to worship and live life together in.

Special thanks to College Press for the opportunity, and to Joe Boyd, Richard Mosqueda, T.D. Oakes, and Ted Beasley for their contributions.

Introduction

One hurried morning I [Rusty] decided to get breakfast on the go. Rather than a bagel from home, I opted for *the bacon, egg, and cheese value meal* from McDonald's. I felt like my arteries had earned it. The good news was that I had a coupon for a free value meal! The bad news was that it was only for a *small* size. Well I was in need of more than eight ounces of coffee, so I decided to pay the extra and upgrade to a large. I approached the counter and ordered my large-sized value meal, handed over my coupon, and watched the proverbial wrench being thrown into the wheels of the cashier's mind. After she stared at the coupon, my order, and me for a considerable amount of time, she came to the conclusion that this was not possible. I assured her that it was. (I after all did do six months time for the golden arches in my day). She reassured me that it was not . . . so I removed money from my pocket to prove to her that I was intending to pay the difference. Well now she was getting frustrated, so she rounded up the manager. I thought, "Finally! We'll get this taken care of." The manager came up to the counter and assured me that this was not going to be possible. I would have to settle for a small. I was amazed at the inability to think beyond the normal system. And I was even more astonished by their persistence to give me something that I didn't want.

As the church moves into the twenty-first century, she is quickly becoming a lackadaisical restaurant that treats the employee's convenience as the top priority and assumes the customer is always wrong. Now, I'm not suggesting we change the menu to cater to what people *think* they want. I'm simply saying that we are failing to connect with the people who are starving for what we have to offer and find too many obstinate employees that stand as roadblocks to what they really need.

> The church is rapidly becoming a lackadaisical restaurant that assumes the customer is always wrong.

What is the role of the church when it comes not only to connecting with people of this age, but also in training them to further the Great Commission? The training manuals and motivational speeches of old are no longer doing the trick. Gone are the days of "rallying the saints around the cross with a chorus of 'Onward Christian Soldiers.'" A polarization has occurred pitting the church at one end and those outside the church at the other. Bridging the gap between the churched and unchurched has become a tougher engineering feat.

The reason for the gradual distancing is the fact that we no longer share the common values of ethics, truth, God, and country regardless of church affiliation, or lack thereof. At one time the only difference between many Christians and non-Christians was a profession of faith in Jesus. But suddenly we are waking up to a different world and sadly the church on the average continues to hit the snooze bar. The truth is that if the church were to suddenly go through a time warp landing us back in the 1950s we would be geared up and ready to take the world by storm—and do so on the cutting edge.

Why is it that the greatest struggle in the North American church is not the quest to reach more people, or even the desire to deepen the ones we have, but rather the divisiveness within? Why does the term "worship wars" keep surfacing? Is it because we have become *consumers* of church rather than *employees*? Is it because we come to church to be an audience rather than a servant? Is it because we have begun to blur the lines between truth and opinion? We take *opinions* on music and worship and canonize them into *truth*. Method reaches the same level as message, and then war ignites. Mike Breaux, senior minister of Southland Christian Church in Lexington, Kentucky said, "I believe my kids need to know 'Rock of Ages' as much as my mother needs to know 'Shout to the Lord.'" I wonder if God is more concerned about people going to hell than about our lack of using eighteenth-century music?

While the church debates the use of drums on the stage, the world is seeking truth elsewhere. While we discuss whether all denominations are equal, the world is finding inclusion in eastern religion. In one breath we criticize Oprah for her show's "Remembering Your Spirit" segment, yet in another breath we vent about the lack of concern of spiritual matters in our world today. We pound our fist in disgust at the world's portrayal of the afterlife in the cinema, but then we scratch our heads thinking that no one cares about his eternal destiny. We criticize the use of the supernatural and miracles on television, but then shrug our shoulders at how the world will never believe that Jesus was more than a man. Could it be that while the world and the church

Could it be that the world and the church stand side by side in areas of need?

are methodologically miles apart, we stand side by side when it comes to our areas of need?

The world is ready to hear our message of mystery, wonder, and healing! The problem is not that the world isn't interested, it's that we aren't listening to their questions. We want to talk about behavior, when Jesus told us two thousand years ago that it begins with the heart. We are children who have forgotten the joy of playing and the brevity of recess because we are preoccupied with arguing who has "cooties."

This book seeks to move out of the arguments and into the solutions. What do we mean by comparing church leadership with herding cats? Sometimes getting a handle on the direction we need to take the church and figuring out what it is the people inside and outside the church are looking for can seem about as feasible as successfully herding cats. What are the methods we might use to connect, while maintaining the integrity of the message that can change lives? What does it take not only to bridge the gap with a new world, but to train leaders to take the church through this new century? There is far too much at stake for us to expect the world to regress in their thinking because we're afraid of progress. How do we connect with a world that is no longer interested in what we have to say, but is asking the questions for which we have the answers? How do we build bridges for the unchurched who do not look like us? How do we craft our sermons to communicate with our postmodern world? What are the new values for postmodern leaders?

We will write as a tag team in the following pages, identifying which of us is writing along the way. When in doubt, Jeff wrote anything cool and Rusty wrote the practical stuff. As we learn some basic herding skills, let's agree to think outside of the box whenever possible. After all, the issue is feeding the spiritually hungry, not arguing the size of a value meal!

I Feel as though I'm Herding Cats!

[Rusty] have to be honest—I hate cats. It's not that I've had some horrific experience of being mauled by a pack of Persians, it's just that I don't like them. Perhaps it has something to do with their uncontrollable roaming around in the middle of the night. Maybe it is their uncanny ability to climb on everything and in everyone in the house. But, the truth probably is that they are completely unwilling to be trained, taught, or led.

Ever met a cat that responds to its name? What about one that plays fetch? I've never seen a cat bring in the morning paper and slippers. The truth is, they have a mind of their own, and an uncoachable one at that.

Well, welcome to the society of cats. Never more in the history of time have we been more independent, mobile, and stubborn. We reject any attempts at boundaries or confinement, and the word "structure" is quickly becoming the proverbial "box we have to think outside of." With all of our pagers, cell phones, and electronic calendars complete with wireless Web you would think it would give us constant guidance in staying on task. But, rather than guiding us, it empowers us. We now have multiple ways of telling other people what to do as we move freely about the country, and just like cats, we do move freely.

Imagine how difficult it would be to try to move a herd of cats from New Mexico to Colorado, as you would a herd of cattle. The movie *City Slickers* depicted three white-collar business men learning how to move a herd of cattle, and it was funny to begin with, but can you imagine watching these guys move a pack of wild Siamese kittens?[1]

This is the feeling that many church leaders are wrestling with right now, only it's not all that amusing. Nursery rooms are understaffed, Bible Studies are left untaught, and countless potential leaders are unable to make commitments due to a need to maintain freedom. How many ministers have heard the words "I'm just too busy," or "I have too many irons in the fire right now," or better yet "Church is something I can hit around once a month"? I actually once heard, "I can't commit to anything because spring is coming, and that's when I start dating again." As a result, ministry is left unfulfilled, spirituality is left in infancy, and souls are left unreached because of our inability to corral people long enough to impact their lives.

> **Souls are left unreached because of our inability to corral people long enough.**

ATTITUDES AND ACTIONS

If it is true that our society is exploring its feline nature, and we have a need to connect with them, we cannot expect them to change their attitudes and actions so that then we can change their beliefs. We need to make some compromises on their behalf.

There seem to be three levels of how we are wired up. And typically the innermost circle affects the outer rings.

The outer circle represents our actions, the middle circle our attitudes, and the inner circle our beliefs. Our beliefs affect our attitudes, which in turn affect how we behave. Think about it: what would have been the best way to change Adolf Hitler? Tell him "No!" or better yet "Think positive!" Maybe it would have been better to attempt to change his belief system, which then would have affected his attitude towards people, and then his actions toward Jews. Our attitudes and actions are a result of our beliefs.

In the early 1900s our western culture as a whole held similar beliefs about religion and behavior. As a result, the main emphasis of the church was to encourage acceptable actions. Much of the preaching and teaching of this time focused on black and white ethics, clean-cut appearances, and the damnation of social evils. "Don't drink, don't smoke, don't chew, and don't go with girls that do."

Towards the middle of the century we began to witness the differing of opinions on the actions of our government and the church. Many in our society were disenchanted with the church for its bigotry, and at odds with the government for its military actions. As a result, we witnessed an emergence of "hippies" who tried to convince us to exchange our attitudes of hatred for those of peace and love. Likewise, several years later the church found great success in shifting its efforts from changing actions to changing attitudes. We were able to build on the fact that for the most part, our society still maintained the same absolutes of God and the Bible. In theory, if we could just convince people of our need to love ourselves like the God of the Bible loves us, then our rediscovered self-esteem would affect our decision-making. For many years this approach worked, and in some segments it still does.

But for the most part, over the past twenty years, society has begun not only to shuck the actions of the moral, and the attitudes of the loved, but also the belief in absolutes. Telling examples of this are always seen in cinema and music, and two examples of art imitating life demonstrate for us how we are living in a different time.

The classic movie of the better part of the twentieth century has always been regarded as *Casablanca*. Bogart and Bergman's characters exercise moral judgment and preserve personal dignity by rejecting their burning passion for each other to maintain the marital integrity between her and her spouse.

Fast-forward to the Academy Awards of 1997. The Oscar goes to . . . *The English Patient*, a drama that ironically depicts a similar situation between two characters who make the exact opposite decision. They choose to reject the notion of marital faithfulness and satisfy their passion for one another. More than just the Academy has given the nod of approval to this type of judgment.[2]

Let's go back to the sixties and the music of that time. Mick Jagger of The Rolling Stones prances back and forth on stage singing the song "Under My Thumb" stating for us how he has proudly taken dominance over a woman in his life. This attitude, though arrogant, depicts an air of esteem.[3]

Travel through time to 1998. A band called The Offspring released a song ironically entitled "Self-esteem," which depicts the singer's woman cheating on him. He continually takes her back, because after all, he doesn't deserve any better.[4] We live in a culture that awards and applauds the actions of immorality and the attitudes of degradation because we have no god bigger than ourselves.[5]

> We live in a culture that awards immorality and degradation.

Suddenly the church finds herself in a position to battle with belief systems. No longer can we simply tell people to "stop acting that way," or "think positive," we must tackle the question that the world shouts back at us when we give these imperatives and that is, "Why?" The kittens have grown up and run away, and the church must decide whether we stand still and yell, "Heel!" or we begin our pursuit for that which is lost and needs to be led—no matter how difficult that might be.

THREE STORIES

He was hot, tired, and sick of public relations. Worse than a day at DisneyWorld with 100 junior high kids, Moses was at his wits' end. If the masses weren't hungry, they were thirsty. If they were eating chicken, they wanted steak. And every time Moses stopped to look at the map, over a million people would ask, "Are we there yet?"

Truth is, Moses had every reason to snap, but he kept his cool for a long time. The first time he informed God that the people wanted water, he did exactly as God instructed: "Strike the rock, and water will flow." So Moses did just that—not out of anger, or even frustration, but out of obedience. He hit the rock. And it worked. The water gushed forth like an open fire hydrant, and the people danced in the street.[6]

So it just makes sense that he should do it the next time they needed water. The people are thirsty, Moses is more than ready to hit something, and so, he approached God looking for the well and a little therapy. But God says this time is different. "Just *speak* to the rock. No need to hit; just verbally address it, and the floodgates will open. Don't use a previous mechanism for your own sanity or for the sake that it worked last time. I asked you to do something different." But Moses said, "We've never done it that way before," and he swung away.[7]

There was a previous time that a weary Moses called upon God. Poisonous snakes had overtaken the camp and the children of Israel were in dire straits. Moses cried out to God for help, as the people were snake bitten and dying. God instructed Moses to create a bronze snake, raise it before the perishing, and to announce to all who looked upon it that they would be healed. And, sure enough, it worked. Those smart enough to trust in God's plan dusted themselves off and walked away.

Well, as you can imagine, as the years went by, that bronze snake grew more and more precious in their sight. I can just see the children of Israel showing up at the tabernacle astonished that it wasn't displayed. Can't you just hear them, "Hey, who covered up the Holy Snake with this big curtain?" "How's a guy to worship if he can't see the bronze god once a week?" "Someone move that big treasure chest out of the way so we can display the savior of our lives." Somehow the mechanism that God had used to bless their lives, had taken the rank of deity. So, God did what we would expect out of a jealous God, he had them destroy the snake. No matter how good this mechanism once was, it was not worthy of such attention.[8]

Years ago a team of missionaries embarked upon foreign soil. They began integrating their lives and religion into the lives and religion of the native people. They told them about Jesus, they taught them about the sacraments, and they explained to them the cross. The missionaries were amazed at how quickly they were able to convert these people. Within no time, the people of the land had erected crosses up around the city. This seemed to please everyone. After all, this is what the missionaries were teaching them: "Look to the cross!"

Years passed, the missionaries moved on, and soon new missionaries entered the village. They were amazed at the number of crosses around the town. In fact, it seemed as if their work was done, until they began hearing the tribal chants of local witchcraft being shouted in adoration to the crosses. With great anxiety they began to remove one of the crosses only to discover all the village's pagan gods hidden behind the beautiful religious carvings. What had once appeared to be conversion, had been revealed as occult idolatry masked by hollow religion. Every time we use what worked yesterday as the "how-to book" on saving lives, every time we allow the mechanisms of old to become equivalent with deity, we move dangerously close to teaching people how to worship hollow crosses while exercising empty religion.[9]

> When we use what worked yesterday as our pattern we move towards empty religion.

HERDING TACTICS

When it comes to herding any type of animal, we know there are a variety of techniques that are beneficial, and others that are not. And just as a shepherd uses a hook to corral the wandering sheep, there are various hooks we use to steer people in the right direction. But, if we are going to begin to wrestle with the belief systems of this new world, there are a couple of herding hooks that have lost their effectiveness and need to be retired.

The first is *nostalgia*. I can remember growing up hearing the old hymns. I learned solid theology and church doctrine in the continuous singing of "The Old Rugged Cross," "Blessed Assurance," and "Wonderful Grace of Jesus." I found songs of comfort that still minister to me in "It Is Well with My Soul" and "What a Friend We Have in Jesus." And I have to admit, there are times when I would prefer to travel down memory lane and soothe my soul with the sweet memories of those melodies. To hear the rhythmic play of the piano while my mind is flooded with images of thunderous revivals and emotional commitments made. But the problem is that they may only soothe *my* soul. And they only minister to those who grew up in the church. If the church is to fulfill the Great Commission, we must start asking the question "What connects with those who aren't here?" rather than "What welcomes nostalgia in the hearts of the saved?"

I'm not suggesting ridding ourselves of those great lyrics; many postmodern churches of today have simply retooled the hymns with relevant music. But the truth is, it does not help the connection process for unchurched people to turn off their twenty-first century music in the parking lot and walk into a room resounding with the sounds of the 1950s just so a few of us can have warm fuzzies. Our equating "good church services" with "nostalgia and reminiscing" is an improper equation.

2   The second hook in need of retirement is *routine*. All of us from time to time are looking for the perfect system. Four laws for evangelism, ten steps to an engaging sermon, five components to vibrant worship, and the funnel of spiritual growth. We feel a sense of accomplishment and closure once we find something that works. It's as if we have a few successes with a process, a couple of encouraging words, and we wash our hands and say, "Well, that's finished." Have we not settled into a new form of liturgy? Routine can cripple us from moving outside the box of religion and into the world of relationships.

Jesus taught us by example the need to do things differently. He played with children, told stories about sheep, used mud as an object lesson, and called thieves and harlots his "ministry team." We even see signs of Jesus knowing how to read and write. Though that seems trivial to us today, Jesus was on the cutting edge of technology of his time. While many could not read or write in his day, he shows evidence of being able to do both.[10] Routine or "church as usual" was not in his vocabulary.

After close observation we may discover that our membership process is outdated. Rather than just immersion and a handshake, some churches are discovering that mandatory classes coupled with immediate connection into service opportunities help people exercise their responsibility of being a member. In doing this they find a place to serve and a community to care.

We may find that our neat conveyor for moving people into a relationship with Christ may actually be too constricting. People today don't always stay in our process. Some are connecting with a community of believers before they ever connect with Christ. Bill Hybels, of Willow Creek Community Church, stated in a leadership seminar that his church had struggled with this idea of routine. It used to be that small groups were only for people who had been attending church services and were now furthering their relationship with Jesus. But now, non-Christian seekers were beginning to bypass church services and to connect immediately in a small group. They saw this as a place to have both their questions answered and their thirst for community quenched. Hybels said that this caused them to rethink their discipleship structure to the point of creating "seeker small groups."[11] Nike summed it up for us years ago with the ad that simply stated "Another day, another hobby." When it comes to methods and mechanisms, they are only as effective as tomorrow's relevance, not yesterday's results.

POOR TACTICS = POOR SHEPHERDS

The unchurched often have a strong distaste for the use of nostalgia and routine, which we tend to overlook. Not only does this alienate the unchurched, but also it stifles the evangelism efforts of our members. The very people we are trying to train and lead are being given the wrong tools to seek the strays. I can recall the dissatisfaction I had in my youth when I finally got up the nerve to invite a friend to church and had to explain or apologize throughout the entire service. The frustration with the lack of creativity and the sense of ancient practices made the two-hour long service difficult to bear.

One of the reasons so many churches are dying is not because the people are not well fed or are ill equipped in the methods of witnessing, it is that no one is saying with wild enthusiasm, "You've got to be a part of this!" We tell our friends about the movie we saw on Friday night and insist they go and see it. We steer the entire carpool off course in order to convince all the riders of the ultimate bagel shop we've discovered. But when it comes to church, we quietly keep it to ourselves with the secrecy of a male knitting club.

> **When it comes to the church, we quietly keep it to ourselves.**

If our weekly church service was designed to connect people to God in a relevant way, we might be amazed at our lack of need for paid advertisements. Rather than spending the church budget on billboards and catchy jingles, we might find that our greatest advertisement is the satisfied customer. I don't mean to simply entertain. Any church that is a circus in order to attract a crowd will have just that: a crowd. The postmodern mind will spot this a mile away. The crowd is not appealing, but a genuine connection to something bigger than they are is.

Let's talk about marketing for a moment. The last time you were on the Internet, how many advertisements did you "close out" in order to get to what you were after? How many digital cameras, trips to Cancun, and magazine subscriptions did you overlook in an effort to read your e-mail? What about on your way to work? How many billboards did you pass by and never even read? What about all the used cars, value meal deals, and people running for city commissioner you overlooked in an effort to get to your job? What about television? Ever channel surf? Between the Internet, billboards, and television, not to mention the junk mail, newspaper, and radio, we encounter thousands of pieces of information each day soliciting our money, time, and trust. We as a society have trained ourselves to overlook them. So what do you think happens when the church advertises through the mechanisms of wristbands, bumper stickers, and radio jingles on Christian radio? The best advertising is the satisfied beggar helping other beggars to find bread.

New Shepherding Hooks

As impossible as it seems to herd cats, there are actually some shepherding tactics that might help. Here are some possible new "hooks" that can help as we begin to connect with these lives that often run astray. The truth is these ideas are nothing new or profound, they are just simply revisited.

The Hook of Purpose

It is so easy to fall into the routine of "doing church" that we forget what it is we are trying to accomplish. Rick Warren, in his book *The Purpose Driven Church*, reminds us of the church's greatest calling: fulfilling the Great Commission while living out the Greatest Commandment.[12] These two life directives give us not only a target, but also the directions for our aim. It is the lost that we pursue and it is love with which we lead. When it comes to using the hook of purpose, we must revisit the rationale for our target. If we view this from a business perspective, let's ask who exactly is the consumer whose needs we are trying to meet?

	Unhealthy Paradigm	Healthy Paradigm
Consumer:	Church Members	Unchurched People
Employees:	Minister	Minister/Church Members
Employer:	Church Board	God

In unhealthy church situations, the only herding going on is trying to please the people who have already accepted Christ and made this their church home. They pay the bills, they dictate the music, they are there to be served by the people they've hired—the ministers. It is the minister's duty to make the hospital calls, lead the Bible studies, and meet the needs of the consumers. Unfortunately this not only exhausts the minister, but it quenches the ability for church members to become the true "priesthood of believers."[13]

Healthy churches that use the hook of purpose know that the true consumers are those people who are not connected to Christ, or better stated, those who are going to hell. They use all their resources, including the efforts of every believer, to meet the needs of the consumer. "What will it take to reach people with the gospel?" is the burning passion in their hearts. They let their passion for the lost overtake their pref-erence for a certain worship style. They work in teams, they open up their homes, and they do what it takes to build bridges with those who have felt alienated by the church in the past. Their purpose is clear and their method is tried and true. Nothing new just renewed.

> Healthy churches let their passion for the lost overcome their preferences on worship style.

The Hook of Grace

In our attempts to keep from condoning sin, we have often condemned those who seek forgiveness and renewal. Do we realize that if statistics are true in our church populace as they are in society, 10% of our congregation has struggled with homosexuality—maybe not practicing, but perhaps private struggles? Do we realize that a large percentage of the people we see on weekends are divorced? Do our "roll call cards" in the pews ask them to identify themselves as single, married, or divorced, and thus remind them of a pain they'd like to forget? Are we sympathetic to the fact that many have grown up with the pain of abuse or the struggle of growing up in a broken home?

We not only alienate and seclude people who have struggled with sin or the effects of sin, but also those who have commonly been overlooked by the church. For instance, do we realize that a large percentage of our people are often single? The U.S. Census Bureau reports that about 40% of people over the age of 18 are widowed, divorced, or have never been married.[14] How do you think they feel when they hear week after week that "Our church loves families," or have to endure a thirteen-week series on marriage, or see a Sunday school class named "Pairs and Spares"? The singles in our church have the ability to be its lifeblood rather than just a holding tank for marriage, children, and then the church board. Our church is filled with those from different walks of life and it would do us well as leaders to use the hook of grace in order to provide healing and purpose.

The Hook of Authenticity

Since we are dealing with a society that has trained itself to overlook hype, fluff, and other sales tactics, the truth stands out like a sore thumb. Do we understand that the people who sit in our church on Sundays desire more to hear how the minister genuinely deals with today's subject matter on a personal level than to hear canned jokes?

Everything about our society screams for us to cut to the chase. The people are hurting and they are struggling, and they need to know how the truth can affect their lives. A preaching professor in college once said, "You can't slit your wrists every week, but it does help to bleed once in a while." This no-nonsense generation wants to hear how we deal with Christianity, how we struggle with the standards of the Sermon on the Mount, and that we find "living like Jesus" difficult as well. Authenticity is the only way that we can communicate with more than words to a society that is beginning to ask questions for which we have the answers.

TIME TO BEGIN HERDING

As difficult as it seems to herd cats, it may seem even more difficult to surrender some of these traditional tactics, take on some new approaches, and begin using new shepherding hooks. This does not mean that we water down the truth, lower the entrance exam, or disregard repentance. It does mean that we remove obstacles in allowing people to experience not only the refining fire of the gospel, but also its healing balm. It is not that any methods we've used in the past are wrong, it's just that they are now irrelevant. This new world requires our dedication to one thing: Will we live in our time, or will we hope that everyone else will join us where we live?

---

[1] *City Slickers*, MGM, 1991.

[2] David Aaron Murray, *First Things*, No. 73, May 1997; *The English Patient*, Miramax, 1996; *Casablanca*, Warner Bros., 1942.

[3] Jagger and Richards, *Under My Thumb*, 1972.

[4] Offspring, *Self-esteem*, 1994.

[5] As told by Dr. Jerry Walls.

[6] Exodus 17:1-7.

[7] Numbers 20:1-12.

[8] Numbers 21:4-9.

[9] As told by missionaries to Mexico City.

[10] Leonard Sweet, *Postmodernity Lecture* (Waco, TX: March 1998).

[11] Bill Hybels, *Leadership Lecture*, Leadership Summit (South Barrington, IL: August, 2000).

[12] Rick Warren, *The Purpose Driven Church* (Grand Rapids: Zondervan, 1995).

[13] Ephesians 4:11-13.

[14] "Campaigns Leave Singles Feeling Lonely," *Lexington Herald-Leader* (Lexington, KY: October 23, 2000).

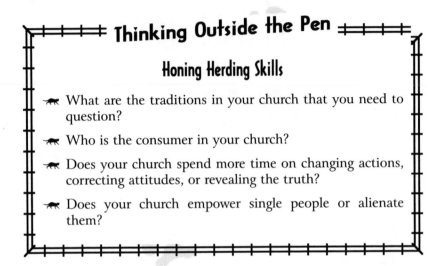

Thinking Outside the Pen

Honing Herding Skills

- What are the traditions in your church that you need to question?

- Who is the consumer in your church?

- Does your church spend more time on changing actions, correcting attitudes, or revealing the truth?

- Does your church empower single people or alienate them?

More than Tattoos and Nose rings

2

When we're herding cats, we're going to shepherd all kinds. We can't expect the unchurched to look like the churched! We learned this in a very graphic way at one of our weekly Young Adult Bible studies. These young men and women have always pursued authenticity and community. One night we decided to do something rather experiential in our attempt to authentically worship as a community of believers. We created a very reflective atmosphere, allowed time for "open mike" discussion, and challenged people to write down on cards particular struggles that they wanted to surrender to God. Open mike opens it up to a variety of characters. Cats come in a variety of shapes, sizes, and "personalities." After an hour of honest and emotional sharing, everyone was instructed to take their cards up to the front of the room and place them in what looked like a birdbath we called an "altar." I [Rusty] watched with tears in my eyes as over 150 people passed by the altar emotionally and physically giving up their sin in a sacrifice to God.

Then, in an attempt to bring completion to their efforts, we took the altar outside, intending to light the cards, and watch our "sin offering" burn up to the heavens. Everyone was in a solemn and somber mood as they encircled the altar. I approached with both a lighter and a sense of standing on holy ground. I lit the cards and watched the authentic confessions of our body of believers begin to turn to flames and then to smoke as they lifted into the night sky. It was truly a special moment. But it was about to get better. As I stood among the people in deep meditation, I noticed a young man in tattered clothes emerging from the crowd. His name was Thomas, and it was his first time there and apparently the last, since I haven't seen him since. But I can tell you this: I will never forget him. He left the crowd, approached the fire, knelt down in front of it, put a cigarette in his mouth, and began the singeing experience of trying to get a light off of the burning sins. I was too stunned to react, and the people who were watching were torn between shock and laughter. After he'd lost his eyebrows and still was unable to light his smoke, he headed over to me. He stuck out his hand. I tried to shake it. He said, "No, I don't want to shake your hand, give me a light." Suddenly my lighter was used for more than just lighting the altar. I began to question: "How do we connect with a twenty-five-year-old guy who hasn't read our handbook of etiquette at church?"

> **How do we connect with a guy who hasn't read our handbook of etiquette?**

The awkward position I was in that night is where many of our churches are today. We are looking at the future of tomorrow in the youth of today and are wondering if their concept of morality and values has been misplaced. Suddenly the phrase "the trouble with kids today" is said with more enthusiasm than in previous years.

We tend to blame all of our trouble on the younger generations. For the past few years we have all been shocked and dismayed by the numerous school shootings at the hands of teenagers. As a result of all of this publicity, do you ever find yourself walking through a local mall seeing adolescents with sagging pants, tattoos, and multiple piercings and feeling afraid? Or what about simple manners? Have you ever stood at the counter in Wendy's and wondered if anyone has ever taught this young cashier not only how to count change, but how to be polite? All it takes is to experience the disrespect for life, the tendency for rage, or the lack of work ethic and discipline and attribute all of society's problems to this generation.

Churches are looking at people like Thomas and are feeling discouraged. Is there hope in the young adults of today to be the church leaders of tomorrow? I'd like to say that the authenticity and vulnerability shown by Thomas are a foundation to be a great leader. But, typically we have three general statements that we use for either explanation of the problem or steps toward a solution.

THEY JUST NEED TO CLEAN UP!

It is true that the majority of people that look bizarre, dress in all black, or have piercings all over their bodies come from the two youngest generations. Previous generations would express themselves by wearing jean jackets or sewing the American flag to their pants. But expression is different today. We have tattoos, tongue studs, and body sculpting (metal objects inserted under the surface of the skin). This generation just needs to clean up and heal up. Right?

Brent is part of the "Goth" (Gothic) community. You've seen this group. They dress in all black, often paint their nails black, and have contrasting pale white skin. And often Brent looks like this. He has multiple tattoos and multiple piercings. His hair, nails, and clothes are all as dark as night. Yet as different as he looks, he is involved in some rather normal behavior. On the weekends he spends time with friends, goes to movies and concerts, drinks coffee. And he even has the same emotional make up. He cries when he's hurt, he's sad when he's lonely, and he desires to be loved. As different as he looks, is he really that different from the rest of us? We all choose different ways to express our feelings.

Many people of the Goth Community are simply expressing their frustration with life in the outlet of their appearance. This looks to me more like people being honest about their despair. Would we rather they cover it up with Dockers and a golf shirt? Granted proper attire and cordial behavior are desired and even honored most places, but is the church failing to seek souls because we are too interested in changing appearances first?

It seems that the reason Jesus erupted with such anger with the moneychangers in the temple was not because he doesn't believe in bookstores in churches, but because he saw obstacles being created for people as they attempted to worship. Elevated prices and monopolized markets caused people seeking the heart of God to find a financial detour in going into His presence. Have we not done the same with the way people look? Should we really demand that people look like us before they come to church, or come to Christ? The truth is that there are just as many lost hearts that dress perfectly acceptably. The issue has never been about dress codes; the issue is about connecting people with the saving gospel of Jesus, and Jesus never fitted someone with a suit before changing his life. Oh, did I mention, Brent is a devoted Christian who has found the hope of Christ and still reaches out to his friends? There is something more to this than just appearance.

The issue has never been about dress codes.

THEY JUST NEED TO GROW UP!

A second claim we often make is that the problems younger generations have are the result of just being young and immature. Perhaps they just don't know any better. There is some truth to this idea. Immature and inconsistent behavior is often a result of age. This is certainly true when it comes to spiritual maturity as well.

One of the traits of these younger generations is that they are spiritually underdeveloped. Many have never been taught anything more than just "go with your feelings." Their idea of a moral code is simply "be true to yourself." With this in mind, many young adults will enter the church with no idea of "how we've always done church." This can take us into uncharted territories that we aren't sure how to navigate.

Our church newsletter published an article several years ago about our Young Adult Ministry. I was quoted as saying that the core belief in our ministry, and the most profound truth anyone can learn, is that Jesus loves him or her. A couple of weeks after this was printed, a young woman named Julie called and scheduled an appointment with me. I had never met nor seen her before, but she had read the article and had a few questions. She was twenty-one years old, bright, cheery, and seemed to have a healthy confidence about her. So it surprised me when she sat down in my office, skipped the small talk, and began with quoting the newsletter. She said, "You said 'Jesus loves people.' Just who is the love for?" She began to cry and plead with me to tell her for whom this mysterious love from Jesus was really intended. "What do I have to do to earn it?" she cried. "How is this possible for everyone? This doesn't make sense," she stated. Any of my textbook answers about the love and grace of God didn't connect with her. Her perspective was skewed from years of people taking from her while simultaneously saying they loved her. Any time anyone had ever said "I love you," it was because they had ulterior motives, so she wanted to know what the catch was. She was a broken and hurting young woman who had never known what true love and grace were all about, and it broke my heart. What bridge do you use to connect two distant islands? We each stood on separate ground. How could I begin to share the concept of grace with her?

Is it fair for me to just assume that Julie will one day grow out of this? She'll meet a nice guy, get married, have a couple of kids, and settle into the church just fine. Is it fair for me to assume that only people Julie's age struggle with these issues? Since our conversation I have encountered similar situations with much older individuals. The effects of sin and lack of trust know no age. Why do we assume that birthdays cure all wounds? In the movie *Hook,* about Peter Pan, there is a scene where Robin Williams is on a business flight. He's trying to get some work done on the plane, but the boy next to him continually disturbs him. After some time of frustration he finally looks at him and says, "Oh, grow up!" to which the boy responds, "I'm seven."[1] The truth is that people today are not necessarily struggling with a *physical* maturity issue but one of *spiritual* maturity. This plague affects more than just the young adults of this society, it is a slow cancer that is attacking us all. It is bigger than just appearance, and it is bigger than just age. And when we say, "Grow up!" they look at us just as that boy looked at Robin Williams.

People are not struggling with physical maturity, but spiritual.

THEY'RE JUST PART OF THAT "GENERATION X" THING!

Information can be both a blessing and a curse. Recently we have been indoctrinated with a steady dose of information that draws lines around age groups and generations. But, like most of our attempts at wisdom, we often come up heavy on breadth, but light on depth. Unfortunately most of the church has heard only enough to allow it to make ignorant comments. We quickly assume that this "Generation X" is simply all of those kids who wear sagging pants, pierce their noses, and get tattoos. So, we end up making comments discussed previously: "Just clean up and grow up!" But the differences between generations, and the nonsynergistic threat they pose are greater now than ever before. Most ministers stand up every Sunday morning and see representatives of four generations. For them to assume that Generation X is a group with no leadership potential, or simply is a group waiting to turn into their parents, is a misunderstanding of who they are and who they always will be. And for them to assume that Generation X is the only generation to struggle with the issues plaguing our world is another misinterpretation of our time and culture. Let's take a brief time-out and refresh our knowledge with the general characteristics of these four generations.[2]

The Builder Generation

This generation is typically categorized as people born before 1945. These individuals generally hold similar moral and ethical beliefs. They endured the depression, World War II, and the continued rise of the industrial revolution. This is predominantly a hard-working, handshake-trusting generation. They know the Bible stories; they even know Bible verses, many of which have been used to teach them the alphabet in public schools. Family values were strong, divorce was down, and patriotism was high during their formative years. An unfortunate characteristic of this generation is that spirituality tended to be surface level and equated only with proper actions.

There is a mysterious cycle in human events. To some generations much is given. Of other generations much is expected. This generation has a rendezvous with destiny.
—Franklin Delano Roosevelt[3]

The Boomer Generation

As a result of the Builder's family focus, an influx of children was born to begin this next generation. The Baby Boomers are generally thought to be those born between 1945–1965. They took a different road than their parents. As a result of Watergate and Vietnam, the government didn't look too appealing. The idea of free love during the '60s gave boomers a new focus—themselves. This was when prayer was removed from school, and soon after, abortion was legalized. Rather than being concerned about family values and community life, this generation pledged their allegiance to individualism. Boomers developed the six-day workweeks, and twelve-hour workdays. As a result, community life, church, and especially God (things that their parents held dear) became spokes on the wheel of their lives, while their own pleasure and interests remained at the hub. Generally speaking, the Boomers were the first to discover burnout in their jobs, their homes, and their personal lives.

> *Imagine there's no heaven;*
> *It's easy if you try—*
> *No hell below us,*
> *Above us only sky.*
> *Imagine all the people*
> *Living for today . . .*
> —John Lennon[4]

The Buster Generation

As a result of abortion, the pill, and the desire not to have a family, the Boomers had fewer children and this generation became known as "the Busters." (AKA Generation X) A busted generation: numerically, emotionally, and spiritually. This is typically categorized as those born between the years 1965–1985. These were the "latchkey" kids because mom and dad were both at work when they got home. These are the "TV" kids because the television became their authority on sex education, relationship advice, and career choices. These are the "whatever" kids because, with a lack of family values being communicated, a growing distrust in politicians, and a "Televangelist" orientation to religion, this generation said "whatever" to most anything of worth. Thus, this generation is the first one to have grown up predominantly without God. It hadn't been important for their parents, so it wasn't important for them to pursue him either. These are also the "angry" kids. They were growing up in broken, abusive, and often-empty homes. They grad- uated from college with degrees that were deemed worth- less by the work force. There were no jobs for them, and suddenly the American dream of having it better than your parents became the American joke. So as a result this generation decided not to live to work, like their parents, but now work to live. They did whatever it took to stay alive and pay for their entertainment and that is all they needed. Rather than collecting "things" they began to collect "experiences." There was a decrease of time at the office, and an increase of time in leisure. The church, for the most part, has found it difficult to connect with people who don't know the story of Abraham and Isaac or the words to "Blessed Assurance" or understand that Jesus Christ is more than a curse word.

> This generation is the first one to have grown up predominantly without God.

> *"Is something wrong?" she said. "Of course there is."*
> *"You're still alive." she said. "But do I deserve to be?"*
> *"Is that the question? And if so, who answers?"*
> —Pearl Jam "Alive"[5]

The Blaster Generation

This next group, the Blasters, also known as "Generation Y," was nurtured more than their parents were, but yet they still lack the understanding of basic moral principles. They have grown up without absolutes, because their parents had none to teach them. This group is typically seen as those born after 1985. They aren't overly interested in turning their minds off to watch television, but rather in turning their minds on by using the Internet. They aren't as angry because they don't expect as much. It is normal for their parents to get divorced. It is normal not to dream as big for the future. Apathy has been the trait they've inherited.

> *Stronger than yesterday,*
> *Now it's nothing but my way.*
> *My loneliness ain't killing me no more;*
> *I'm stronger*
> —Britney Spears, "Stronger"[6]

Back to the issue at hand. When we quickly assume the problem with our society is a particular generation, then we are stating that we expect them to begin to act like another generation. It is not fair for us to say that one generation is closer to God than another, but what we can say is that some generations are more predisposed to the gospel. The fact is that there is a struggle for the church to build a bridge to the latter two generations, and expecting them to grow up and turn into Boomers so we can use our old techniques is lazy. Or worse, to assume that we must convert them to being Boomers or Builders first and then connect them to Christ is simply not biblical.

There is a struggle for the church to bridge generations.

The real problem here is bigger than we'd like to think. It is most prevalent in the recent generations, but it affects us all. It's not about appearance, it's not about age, it's not even about generation; it is about a mind-set. Our culture has been gradually ushering in a new mind-set and belief system whether we recognized it or not. We have been slowly moving out of a time called "Modernity," and into a time called "Postmodernity." Mike Starkey summarized it well in his work *God, Sex, and the Search for Lost Wonder*:

> Many thinkers are increasingly dividing the history of the West into three eras: the premodern (up to the eighteenth century), the modern (from the eighteenth

century to somewhere around the late 1960's or early 1970's) and the postmodern (the present era). The main characteristic of the postmodern era is that all the big ideas—faiths, philosophies and "isms"—of the previous two eras have collapsed. In religious terms, if premodernity was the era dominated by a single religion—Christianity—modernity was dominated by a single dogma—secular progress. What then of postmodernity? The postmodern world is motivated by a single impulse—personal choice.[7]

The implications from this will affect everything the church does in her efforts to connect not just lost young adults, but even more, a lost world in general.

NOT AN AGE—A MIND-SET

While sitting in a Sunday school class I came face to face with this. We were discussing the Passion Week, specifically Jesus cursing a fig tree. It was then we were interrupted by the words, "I don't believe that. Jesus wouldn't curse a tree for not having fruit." The belief that many of us held of the inerrancy of Scripture was apparently not held by all in the room. The strange thing was that we weren't in Seattle, we were in Kansas. And this wasn't a "GenXer" with a nose ring, he was a sixty-two-year-old elder! In our tripping over terms like appearance, age, and generation, we forget that we all not only live in a culture that constantly is deconstructing God, but it affects us all.

What we are dealing with in our culture is not just an age distinction; it's not just the kids that have the trouble. It's a mind-set. Something radical happened between the generations of the Boomers and the Busters that had been brewing for centuries. It is a major shift in our society, and the last time we saw it, we were moving from the agricultural age into the industrial age. Long before even the Builders were on the scene, the world transitioned into the "modern" age. Modernity brought with it a promise of prosperity, knowledge, and power through the means of an industrial revolution. Suddenly through the absolutes of the wisdom and science of man, we could master our health through medicine, we could defy gravity and speed with planes and automobiles, and we could conquer our emotions by blending pop psychology with our religion. Living in the modern age promised us the absolute truth that we had everything under control.

Over the past thirty years we have begun completing a major shift in our world. Not only were we ushering in new generations, but along with them a new culture. We moved from the industrial age into the information age. Suddenly it wasn't about our strength as much as it was about our minds. The Internet did for our age what the printing press did for the previous age. Along with this shift in our economy and vocational direction, came a shift in our mind-set regarding science. Science was what we put our trust in, but when cancer couldn't be cured, and Dr. Spock didn't fix our kids, we began to disregard the notion of absolute truth in this field. When Marxism failed to be what it had promised to one side of the world, and capitalism failed to provide the American dream for everyone, plus the scandals of the inner workings of politics began to be revealed, we naturally disregarded the notion of absolute truth in government. And sadly religion, more specifically, the church, was viewed in the same light. When Darwinism won the monkey trials, when legalism failed to provide the freedom that only grace can offer, and when our Televangelists publicly fell to immoral behavior, people began to disregard the notion of absolute truth in the church and her God. Postmodernity dawned.[8]

Welcome to a world whose only absolute is that there are none. G.K. Chesterton began to diagnose this[9] in his work *Orthodoxy*. He states, "A man was meant to be doubtful about himself, but undoubting about the truth; this has been exactly reversed." Anything is accepted, even if it doesn't make sense. In this type of culture the greatest sin is *intolerance*. You can maintain all the beliefs you want, as long as they don't exclude anyone else's beliefs.

What does this mean for us today? Quite simply postmodernity will impact us all, regardless of age and appearance. You will have sixty-year-old people who have been affected by postmodernity as much as you will have twenty-five-year-old young adults who have only known postmodernity. Leonard Sweet refers to anyone born before 1962 as an immigrant, and anyone born after as a native. The natives of postmodernity obviously are more affected by its values, but that doesn't mean the immigrants haven't achieved citizenship.[10]

Welcome to a world whose only absolute is that there are none.

There are those who have become "postmodernists." They buy into their culture and its beliefs and make a conscious decision to appropriate these beliefs in their lives. Then there are the people who are simply affected by postmodernity. They don't necessarily subscribe to the belief system of no absolutes and a deconstruction of God, but they are affected by it. They catch themselves saying, "Well, to each his own," or "Just because it's wrong for you doesn't mean it's wrong for me." They begin to view bedrock truths as mere philosophy or even fable. In some ways we are all affected by this culture.[11]

The question is, How do we continue the mission of the church in this day and age? Should we simply try to convert the natives to the immigrant's way of thinking? Teach them about the old country, with the old techniques? Do we try to convert postmodernists and those whose mind-sets have been affected by postmodernity to modernity? Convince them of the absolutes of science, God, and country, the right way to behave and proper attitudes to have so that they are ready for the gospel? Obviously this is not part of the Great Commission. Jesus did not die on the cross, resurrect, and leave us with the charge to transition people to a more favorable culture or philosophy. The only absolute we need to convince them of is the absolute of the gospel.

Jesus has called us to take the gospel to every tribe, nation, and culture regardless of whether it was more conducive to do so in the modern time. We must move beyond waiting for everyone to become white, middle-aged, yuppies on a career track, complete with mission statement and daily planner. The gospel extends to all people groups, and it does not require us to become Boomers, Builders, or even Busters but Christ-followers.

> The only absolute we need to convince them of is the absolute of the gospel.

Jesus Christ is the same yesterday, today, and tomorrow, and he certainly can relate and exist within a postmodern culture without first connecting to modernity. The question is how? How do we take people with a postmodern bent, reach them with the gospel, and then train them to be the leaders of the church of tomorrow?

BAD SIGNS

Unfortunately the church often impedes the progress of postmodern people in their quest for connection and truth. There are a few signs that hang around our churches that constantly call people to modernity first and then to Christ.

Proper Dress Required

Granted appropriate dress is required in certain jobs, in certain restaurants, and even in certain events. It makes sense that the church should "offer our best to the Master." But, this culture tends to shun anything of arrogance or self-glorification.

Many of the people we need to reach don't have jobs that require a high dress standard, nor eat in fancy restaurants, nor attend any events that segregate by attire. They are sick of the materialism they saw in the '80s and are more interested in authenticity.

One of our Adult Bible Fellowship groups meets on Sunday morning. They noticed a certain new couple had stopped attending, so the teacher decided to give them a call. After several probing questions about their desire not to come back, they finally said, "We don't feel like we dress nice enough to come." I think "the Master" is more interested in this couple than he is in the group's "proper attire." When we communicate to people that nothing but coat and tie will do for us, we tell people in a postmodern world that there are certain standards you have to meet before you become eligible for truth and community, specifically, Jesus and the church.

Nothing Less Than Perfection

Our culture is beginning to embrace its brokenness. Never before have we been so public about the therapist we see, the twelve-step group we attend, or our need for certain diet plans. We are consumed with our weaknesses. Unfortunately, people see in many churches false perfection. Sometimes a well-detailed and programmed service provides an excellence that is glorifying to God. And it should. But when excellence turns into perfectionism—any mistake is frowned upon, spontaneous comments are scripted and rehearsed, and messages are filled with self-glorifying comments and degrading reprimands of the congregation and world—we have begun to display this sign. A guitar string breaking, a voice cracking, the minister discussing his struggles with today's text, all reaffirm to people that Jesus can use anyone, especially the imperfect.

> Jesus can use anyone, especially the imperfect.

Limited Availability for Service

The loneliest person in our church is that single young female artist. She can't serve as an elder in most churches because she isn't married or male. She is left out of many decisions because, being female, she isn't invited to the meetings. And because she doesn't sing, she is left out of the choir. We tend to only permit people to serve in the boxes we have created. We force people into the nursery, the choir, or the church board and disregard those who have so much potential, talent, and time. If a person has artistic ability, it is the church's job to help her discover how her talent can be used as an act of worship. We assure her that she can be a vital part of what goes on around here, help her build a team, and see to it that they succeed.

Things Are More Important Than People

Our church recently began a building campaign. Some of our elders went to each Adult Bible Fellowship class and cast the vision for what we thought God had called us to do. It was interesting to hear some of the questions. One of our classes filled with people from the Builder generation asked, "Will the parking lots be big enough?" Yet, one of our classes filled with young couples from the Buster generation asked, "Will there be enough green space and playground equipment?" Not that there is anything wrong with parking lots, but it does indicate the focus is changing. This culture is focused more on people and beauty than they are on things. God does call churches to grow, and bigger buildings are sometimes needed, but the question becomes how do we use the buildings. Are they for display only, filled with memorials and untouchables to the point that it becomes a museum? Or are they user friendly and people targeted? Do we make our main focus missions and allow God to use the synergy from large gatherings to generate money and resources for outreach efforts overseas and downtown? Do our people know that we want them on short-term mission experiences as much as we want them in a midweek Bible study? Are we too consumed with things, programs, and procedures rather than people?

Several weeks ago after one of our services I stood talking with a couple of young adults. They were new to the church and hadn't had the course on dos and don'ts. They were fresh out of the world of wild living and individualism; the icons and traditions of the church were completely foreign to them. As we spoke, I noticed that one of these guys had picked up the basket of communion wafers and began to snack on them. My fundamentalist side wanted to cry out "Hey, buddy, that's the body of Christ, don't touch!" But then I realized that he'd probably heard that enough from the church. The role of the church should not be to expect the unconnected to meet standards before introducing them to Jesus, but to extend grace that overlooks appearance, age, generational differences, and especially ignorance of church procedures.

[1] *Hook*, Amblin Entertainment Productions, 1991.

[2] Generational studies are numerous and many have influenced these observations. A few sources to be noted: Gary L. McIntosh, *Three Generations* (Grand Rapids: Revell, 1995); Leonard Sweet, *Postmodern Pilgrims* (Nashville: Broadman & Holman, 2000); Mike Starkey, *God, Sex & the Search for Lost Wonder* (Downers Grove, IL: InterVarsity, 1997); Stanley Grenz, *A Primer on Postmodernism* (Grand Rapids: Eerdmans, 1996); Dawson McAllister, *Saving the Millennial Generation* (Nashville: Thomas Nelson, 1999).

[3] Ken Baugh and Rich Hurst, *Getting Real* (Colorado Springs: Navpress, 2000), p. 40.

[4] John Lennon, *Imagine*. Bag Productions, Inc. 1971.

[5] Pearl Jam, *Alive*, 1991.

[6] Rami and Max Martin, *Stronger*, 2000.

[7] Mike Starkey, *God, Sex*, p. 99.

[8] Though this proposition has been influenced by numerous conversations, lectures, and authors, the strongest contributors are Ken Baugh and Rich Hurst, *Getting Real*, and a Web essay by Mark Driscoll, *Postmodernity*, www.marshill.fm.

[9] G.K. Chesterton, *Orthodoxy* (New York: Image Books, 1959), p. 31.

[10] Leonard Sweet, "Who Moved My River?" Part 1. Off the Map Evangelism Conference 2000. Vineyard Community Church, Cincinnati, OH.

[11] This theory comes from the teaching of Dr. John Castelein, professor at Lincoln Christian Seminary.

Thinking Outside the Pen

Honing Herding Skills

- What are the absolutes that the church must maintain in an age of tolerance?

- What are the prejudices against generations that you have held or noticed?

- What are some "bad signs" that hang around your church?

- What are some new "tools" that could help your church reach this culture?

Moving from the Empty Tomb to the Rugged Cross

ave you ever tried looking through the eyes of a cat? Have you noticed the differences in perspective between a cat and its owner? Take ordinary household items for example. You see a wool sweater from a pricy department store; your cat sees the best bed money can buy. You see a nicely re-covered armchair; your cat sees a first-class scratching post. Herding cats, like working with postmoderns, requires that herders acquire a new perspective.

The postmodern world sees the Bible and traditional Christianity and theology differently than Christians do. As we indicated in chapter one, cats do not respond to our every command. They may not answer when called by name! We may need to change our terminology as well as the way we present the old story. It may look completely foreign to the image we would expect.

Janet walked into my [Jeff's] office one afternoon. She had requested the meeting after attending worship and Bible study at our church for six months. We exchanged small talk and I could tell that she was nervous. She asked about how I had entered the ministry and why I had chosen to take this particular vocation.

When she began to feel comfortable with me, I asked her the question, "So what did you want to talk to me about?" She explained that she had a lot of questions about the church, the Bible, and Jesus as the Son of God. She explained to me that she didn't necessarily believe in all the teachings in the Bible. She didn't believe that homosexuality, abortion, and sex outside of marriage were wrong, all the things that I had taught about since she had been attending. She told me that she believed that everyone would one day get to heaven and that God is a loving God and would never condemn any-one to hell. I asked her what she thought about Jesus. She told me that he probably was a good man, with a lot of useful teaching to share with the world, but that to expect all people to believe in him in order to "get right" was a completely ridiculous concept. After all, how are the people in Africa ever going to get to heaven if they never hear about Jesus? Janet went on for a half hour telling me why she didn't agree with anything our church was teaching about God and the Bible, a church that she had been regularly attending and participating in for half a year.

I interrupted her and asked her this question, "What in the world are you doing here?" Her reply almost knocked me out of my chair. She said, "I am looking for something, and this is as close to finding it as I have ever been." She said, "I sit in church every week and cry, sometimes uncontrollably. I love the friends I have made here, and I am desperately looking for answers to the questions that I have about God."

For the next hour she told me her story—a story that included sexual and mental abuse as a child and teen in her home and with close relatives; how she grew up in a cult, with parents who were drug and alcohol abusers. She explained how she and her mother left her father and the cult behind to start a "new life." She told me of her siblings, one who had become a Mormon and another who was a Jesus freak, and how for so long she had tried to find God with no luck at all. She had bounced in and out of churches for the past seven or eight years and always found people who wanted to "convert" her to their religion, but never really cared to get to know her. She had finally found a place in this church where she could be who she was and take a good, honest look at who God was and how she might relate to him.

One year later, Janet still attends our church. She is still a regular participant in a small group Bible study, and she has yet to accept Jesus Christ as her personal Lord and Savior. Now many of you reading this book right now are probably questioning my ability to "close the deal." How can any self-respecting minister let an unbeliever sit in his church week in and week out without calling her to accept Christ? I have even thought that of myself over the past year and a half. Janet and I still meet together and talk, and she is growing. I pray that one day I will be able to talk with her as more than a friend, but as a sister in Christ.

Our cultural climate demands that we change the way in which we present Jesus to people and how we relate to the Janets of this world. We must recognize how they perceive Jesus as their Savior and us as the church.

A BURDENED PEOPLE

The emerging postmodern world is full of Janet stories— young men and women who are struggling to find their identities in adulthood apart from the identities their parents gave them as children. They are a people on a journey to find significance and meaning in their lives and in the world around them. Consider this. They grew up as the most aborted generation in history. *They have no value in the world.* They found themselves living in homes with only one parent. *They found no love in the world.* They were promised wonderful careers and success if they would only go to college and follow in their parents' footsteps. *They found no future in the world.* They were told that God was the answer to all of their problems and yet all they saw in God was religious ceremony and hypocritical nonsense. *They have no hope in the world.* Everyone has let them down and now they are on their own to make sense of a seemingly senseless place. They are a burdened people.

They are on a journey. Interestingly, that journey has brought them to consider spiritual matters, to ask the tough questions about God, hoping that he would have an answer to satisfy their longings. For those of us in the modern church, it would seem logical that any spiritual discovery would begin with the God of the Bible and the church. So we wait expectantly every Sunday morning at the front door of the church, in our Sunday spiffs, with our name tags in place, waiting for our children, our lost sheep to come home. And they don't come.

We assume that they will find their way home to our church—they have been here many times—and yet we wonder to ourselves, why is our congregation getting older every year? Where are all of the young people? Why do our children grow up, move away, and never come back? This collection of humanity, in all its splendor, is searching out a place to have its heart's cry heard, but our churches aren't the places to have that cry answered.

Why do our children gow up, move away, and never come back?

The Joy of the Journey

Though Jesus is the only way to God, it would seem that the way in which people are coming to accept Jesus as their Lord is changing. Not that it has altogether changed, but that it is certainly not the same way for everyone anymore. It would seem that the "point in time" conversion of old is being replaced with a more relationship-driven, experiential model of faith sharing that allows individuals to exist and participate in Christian community without having accepted Christ themselves. The modern church's method of evangelism and discipleship is to show someone Jesus and then help her find a church in which she can grow. The postmodern method is to help people find a community to grow in and then show them Jesus. It is almost as if postmoderns convert to the Christian community before they accept Jesus. If this is the case, it would appear that the way of the "altar call" and emotional salvation plea from the preacher needs to change.

The postmodern method is to help people find a community and then show them Jesus.

Suffering Savior or Risen Lord

If we believe that the way in which postmoderns come to Christ and to the church is different than that of previous generations, then we need to rethink the process of conversion that we lead them through. Now, we would not suggest that Jesus has to change in some way for postmoderns to accept him, but we certainly need to show him to them in a way in which they can relate.

The modern church has been very successful at presenting the person of Jesus to the unbelieving world in a way that emphasizes his resurrection victory. We present Jesus as our risen Lord. We celebrate Jesus, who has defeated death, who has risen from the grave, and who reigns victoriously in heaven. Our music reflects that in the light, airy, victorious melodies that we sing on Sunday morning. Our worship settings are bright and big, with color-coded hallways, signs, name tags, and bulletins. *We construct worship venues that project an air of religious superiority to the rest of the world.* Our preaching emphasizes the victorious life that we can live with Jesus. We preach how all of life will make more sense if we would only have a relationship with Christ. All of these things are true, and they work with people who relate to their world through a lens of victory. The concept of a Risen Lord who has defeated death is a partially accurate picture of who Jesus is and one that has worked well in the modern church.

The postmodern church is a church that is embracing Jesus as a crucified Savior. Jesus is being preached in barns and bar rooms, in candle-lit, smoke-filled, carpet-stained warehouses and storefronts that were once deemed unusable. Bulletins are now programs. The place of worship may be a room that is used for ten other ministries during the week. The members and seekers meet in people's homes; they share meals and expenses together. They seem to enjoy going to church any time after 5:00 p.m. and only if they don't have to dress up. We are dealing with a generation that has a hard time relating with a victorious and conquering Savior. They have a hard time seeing Jesus as their risen Lord. Everything in their world suggests that this is not possible. They can relate, though, to a Savior who has experienced the rejection and heartache that they have experienced. A Savior who has had everyone who was close to him abandon him in his time of greatest need. A Savior who had to endure a less than idyllic life, and a man who, in spite of all that was against him in his life, found peace and contentment in his relationship with his heavenly

> **We are dealing with a generation that has a hard time seeing Jesus as their risen Lord.**

Father. This is a man that postmoderns can relate to, and it is the picture of Jesus that we as a church need to present to them.

THE COMMUNITY OF BELIEVERS

Not only is the postmodern perception of Jesus different from the generations before them, their perception of the church is also quite different. To modern believers the church is the place where they are able to participate in the fellowship of the saints, to gather with other Christians who believe and live the same way that they do. Its organizational structure revolves around the large, weekly gathering of Christians. Because of that, churches have been a place of meeting. A place that has an identified building, address, and letterhead to legitimize its existence. While the postmodern church still gathers for and cherishes the large, weekly worship time, it is not necessarily the most prominent expression of the church. The postmodern church best expresses itself in smaller, community groups of people that resemble the larger gathering of the modern church. Because of their desire for a relational connection, the small, house church seems to be the most effective way to reach out and to share the relational discipleship model of Jesus. It is in this setting where needs are shared and met, where intimate prayer time takes place, where social needs are fulfilled, and where worship, service, and ministry are expressed. The emerging generations value the community aspect of the church, the one aspect that has lost some of its importance in the modern church.

PROCESS OVER PRODUCT

If we are to reach the postmodern mind, to share a new expression of Jesus to the unbelieving world, then we must be prepared to embrace a different, more relational model of evangelism. As we learn to understand and embrace the way in which postmoderns process truth, we will quickly see that our current methods of evangelism will most likely fall on deaf ears. Postmoderns process truth relationally, making them different in many ways from the generations that have come before them. The modern church has presented Jesus logically and systematically in a way that argues Jesus as the most reasonable alternative to the world needing salvation. It is a form of evangelism that produces a response. It demands that a person make a decision either for or against Jesus in the moment. While the point-in-time, crusade type of evangelism has worked in the past, it may not be the most effective way for the church to continue its bold proclamation of Jesus in the future. While we would not suggest an alteration of the message of hope and salvation through Jesus Christ alone, we would like to suggest a more relational, process-driven method—a relational model that recognizes the individual and his pain and struggle in this world and Jesus as his shepherd, comforter, healer, and companion in this life's journey.

Jesus, after his resurrection, appeared to two men as they were traveling along the road to Emmaus. He joined them in their journey and participated in their conversation as they walked together on the road. He listened to what they had to say, and even though they were slow to come to a complete understanding of what the prophets and Moses spoke of, they eventually were able to embrace Jesus in their journey. This is quite a different experience from what the apostle Paul experienced on his journey to Damascus. God grabbed him in a moment and snatched him from a life of persecuting the church and turned him around. Both experiences were the same in that they brought about salvation to the people who met Jesus. Both experiences were also very different in that the method of the presentation of the truth varied greatly.

Throughout the Old and the New Testaments, we find that God called different people at different times in a variety of different ways. While the end result was the same, the value in God's eyes was not necessarily the process of salvation, but the product or the salvation experience itself. To that end, we must constantly remind ourselves that our method of sharing the truth of salvation in Christ alone can never become as sacred as the message. It is evident that the point-in-time experience of Paul is an effective method of sharing Jesus with people. While it may still have its use, it isn't the only way by which an effective gospel presentation can be made. The church must recognize this change and embrace whatever form (within obvious reason) is necessary to continue to share Jesus with the unbelieving world.

> Our method of sharing the truth must never become as sacred as the message.

COMMUNITY TO CHRIST

We have a growing population in our church: people who have yet to accept the tenets of Christianity, but are investigating the authenticity of our community. Like Janet, they are unwilling to make the jump to belief in Jesus as their Lord and Savior, but for different reasons enjoy the comfort and authenticity of this group of people who do believe.

We are in the process of rehabbing an old church building that was given to us in order to move our congregation. We committed early on in the process that much of the labor would be supplied by people in the church. Every Saturday for the last three months we have been working to clean up this building. I had noticed a particular young woman who had been coming to work on a regular basis and I didn't know who she was. After a little investigation, I found out that she wasn't a believer but was a coworker of one of our members. She had been attending regularly with her friend. I was amazed that someone who had no "official" tie to our congregation would give up multiple Saturdays to help in rehabbing a building for a church that preached a message that she had yet to accept.

Then I realized that this person was doing some serious spiritual investigating. She was investigating the validity of Christianity, but not through theological questioning. She was forming her opinion relationally, based on her interaction with Christians. We have more and more people who are attending Bible studies and worship services so that they can meet people. They are then making their decision about the validity of the gospel after they see it lived out in the lives of Christians. Their conversion is first to the community and then secondly to the person of Jesus.

Yet our emphasis in programming in our church continues to focus on information. We prioritize our ministry structure based heavily on the dissemination of information. All the while, we have people who just want to "hang out" and meet people so that they can see our theology at work.

In a recent staff meeting, I wanted to review our purpose and values. Do a little checkup on how we were doing, what we needed to change, and what was going well. It was brief and to the point. Our purpose, as we see it, is to facilitate opportunities for pre-Christians to experience the truth of the gospel lived out among Christ-followers. Ours is a relational evangelism.

SHAME TO SIN

Ask a person today if there is evil in the world and he will immediately respond with a yes. Most everyone believes that we live in a world plagued by evil people and evil philosophies. Ask the same person if he sins, and he will probably become defensive, agitated, and try to come up with an "all people are basically good" kind of song and dance. You see, postmoderns think that there is evil in the world; they just don't think that mankind, specifically themselves, has any-thing to do with it. They do not want to take any personal responsibility for the evil of the world. Our challenge as a church will be to teach them about sin in a way that allows them to personalize it. Salvation isn't neces-sary for people who don't sin. Our goal then shouldn't be to try to convince them that they are sinners, but first to share with them what sin is. What we are dealing with in many respects is a faulty perception of sin and thus a rejec-tion of it based on the faulty perception. The church needs to teach a right understanding of sin so that we can help them see their need for Jesus.

> Post-moderns think there is evil in the world, but that they don't have anything to do with it.

The messages that boom from many pulpits often deal with condemnation of sinners. We doom abortionists; we blast homosexuals as abominations. God hates divorce, and we label those sexually active outside of marriage as depraved. These are the facts of the case and they are undisputed. The problem with this attack on the sinner is that most of the people that we will minister to in the coming years will have participated in these acts or are closely acquainted with our list of condemned people. Why would someone who is not saved want to come to you to ask a question about God when all you do is attack who she thinks she is? We are no longer addressing a Republican crowd on Sunday morning who will cheer wildly when we use the Democrat party to illustrate a negative point. People who are coming to our churches need to see that Jesus doesn't care about our sin as much as he cares about our soul. Jesus did not condemn the Samaritan woman at the well, he embraced her. It was after she had developed a relationship with the Christ that she was able to see her own spiritual poverty.

I am convinced that when people see themselves compared to the holiness of God, they will be broken before him.

We must first show them Jesus. We spend too much time trying to clean people up before they can come to Christ. Through our preaching and teaching, it is assumed that most everyone in the room has it together. Is it any wonder that people conclude, "This is no place for me"? I know that when people get to know Jesus, I won't have to convince them to stop having sex outside of marriage. The Holy Spirit living in them is given for that purpose. I know I won't have to convince them to stop cheating people in their business; God's Word makes that plain. My responsibility is to show them the Christ, the Savior who came to rescue the wretched and the broken and the spiritually poor from eternal separation from the Father. Those are the people who sit in out churches week in and week out. How do we get postmoderns to embrace healthy, God-honoring relationships? Show them Jesus. How do we get them to take responsibility for their actions? Show them Jesus.

Postmoderns will come to grips with the sin in their lives. They are a generation in so much pain, and they need to be brought to their knees in desperation because of their irresolvable condition before God. More than that, they need to see Jesus. Jesus will send them to their knees. He will be the catalyst for change in their behavior. And only he will help them see what sin does to the Father.

We need to stop shaming people to the point that they are afraid to share with anyone at church what is going on in their lives. Postmoderns have plenty of peers who will affirm their life-style choices and embrace them for who they are. They don't need to sit in church and hear how bad God thinks they are. They need to hear how much God loves them, and they need to see it displayed through the hands and mouths of his followers. The conviction of sin will come, as it always does when people meet Jesus.

> They don't need to sit in church and hear how bad God thinks they are.

POSTSCRIPT

Janet is desperate to make a connection—to connect with people who understand her struggle. She also wants answers. She would never admit it to my face, but I can see that she senses the community of believers that she is hanging around might finally be a place for her to ask some of those questions and find some of those answers. We have our work cut out for us, though. Janet is guarded and will remain that way until we can prove that we are not like those "other churches." She needs to see that our goal isn't to make her look good on the outside, but to help her deal with the pain that is destroying her on the inside. My Savior is just what she needs. He knows her pain and will take up her cause. He can offer her the rest she needs from the burdens she is bearing.

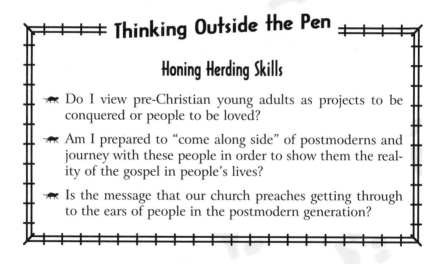

Thinking Outside the Pen

Honing Herding Skills

🐾 Do I view pre-Christian young adults as projects to be conquered or people to be loved?

🐾 Am I prepared to "come along side" of postmoderns and journey with these people in order to show them the reality of the gospel in people's lives?

🐾 Is the message that our church preaches getting through to the ears of people in the postmodern generation?

It's Not Just Three Points and a Poem Anymore

4

While completing a sermon brief for an expository preaching class in college I [Rusty] filled in the blank marked "State Intended Audience:" with the words "Typical church audience." Several weeks later I received that same paper back with these unforgettable words written in red: "There are no 'typical' church audiences." This overgeneralization is a common, repeated mistake. The ability to correctly and precisely identify the needs and characteristics of an audience is an art perfected only through discipline and practice.

Back to the ranch as we rub some more fur. Cats in general are disciplined in their own world, but their sets of needs are different from ours. Humans cannot organize cats. Trying to outline a cat's program or schedule its day would be an exercise in futility. Cats are characteristically and typically picky and independent. Herding cats requires a totally innovative approach! Cats require individual attention to detail and custom-tailored care.

It wasn't too long after learning that important lesson that I found myself forgetting it. I was scheduled to speak at a high school week of camp and was preparing a message on authenticity. The refrain I wanted to stress was the idea of "dropping your mask" and it just so happened that I had a perfect story to illustrate this point.

When I was in junior high and still dressing up for Halloween, one year I chose to dress up as *E.T.*, the adorable alien from the popular Stephen Spielberg movie of the previous summer. I painstakingly designed a custom-made costume out of chicken wire, papier-mâché, and brown paint. With the addition of some scuba flippers for my feet, I had successfully transformed myself into an extraterrestrial. Yet as good as my mask was, it didn't beat out the girl dressed as an angel. It was devastating, but perfect for illustrating my point. In fact, I was so excited about the story that I chose to use it as the introduction and conclusion of the message. I would tell part of it, leave them spellbound with suspense, preach the text, and then return to the story at the climax of the sermon. I was already preparing for a call from "Preaching Today."

The sermon was clean, clear, and delivered without a hitch. I walked off the stage preparing to sign autographs, but instead, I was greeted with a high school student asking me the question, "Who's *E.T.*?" In all my preparation I had forgotten to identify my audience. They were in preschool when *E.T.* was popular, and thus had no idea what I was talking about. The sermon fell not on deaf ears, but unknowing ears. Have you ever wondered why our attempts at communicating the gospel sometimes fall short?

> The sermon fell not on deaf, but on unknowing ears.

Understanding your audience has never been more crucial than in the postmodern age. Assuming that everyone has the same spiritual acumen is as arrogant as expecting everyone to have a working knowledge of *E.T.* In doing so we fail to take into account an audience's age, education, church background, or lack thereof. Preaching in today's culture requires that we understand the effects that postmodernity has had on society.

CHARACTERISTICS OF THIS NEW AUDIENCE
Information à la Carte

School is designed to impart information at a rate and speed in relation to the student's age and ability. You never learned algebra in kindergarten nor archery in second-grade physical education class. And the intricate part of this process was the teacher. There was always an authority figure that dispensed the information and training in proportion to the student's age. It was her decision. In fact I can recall sitting in a history class in eighth grade curious for further detail into the strategy of World War II only to have the teacher tell us we'll study that in high school. Sure, I could have gone to the library and researched a stack of encyclopedias, but there was nothing intriguing about study. I wanted to be painted a visual picture through story and facts. There was one person with access to the knowledge, and she was only dispensing it in proportion to age.

Today is different. With the ability to access the Internet, suddenly people of all ages are able to find whatever they want in a very engaging display. What used to be a child sitting in a class hearing one thing then going home to study that one thing by himself or with the assistance of a parent, is now a child coming home to the computer and, with the community of friends, she retrieves whatever information she desires.[1] Suddenly learning requires no authority figure. As a result, the respect of teachers, as well as preachers, will become more based on how these authority figures help students process what they've already learned. They are no longer relying on us for facts and figures; they can get those. Nor are they held captive to our dispensing of information at a rate we think they can handle; they get it themselves. What is frightening is to wonder from what vantage point they will be instructed.

Breadth, but Not Depth

The power that people will now have to become a virtual "expert" in everything will become a false sense of security. Even though they may know many facts, they may not have any wisdom. *Processing* the information is now the problem. I have many conversations with young adults who profess to know exactly what I am talking about because they have seen it on the Web. The problem is that they have seen one viewpoint regarding the issue and have not wrestled with what the truth really is. It's one thing to say, "I've heard God was unjust and unloving in the Old Testament"; it's another to say, "I've researched it from all angles." As years go by and as people's knowledge base continues to broaden but not deepen, the minister will begin to see more and more pseudointellectualism staring back at him in the congregation. A new type of arrogance will begin. Rather than "I don't need this," the claim will be "I already know this." The preacher in this age will have to create new tension that says, "There is more to this than what meets the eye."

Rather than the claim "I don't need this," it will be, "I already know this!"

ADD+ADHD+Remote Controls

Ever been in a conversation and found yourself thinking ahead of the person? You know where he is headed so you begin nodding hoping he will speed up so you can then talk. We are constantly trying to speed everything up. We read mail and hold meetings. We eat breakfast, apply make up, and talk on the cell phone—while we drive. And as we continue to use computers to communicate, our ability to maintain a conversation in a natural way will diminish. Social skills will become awkward, and we will view talking like we view e-mails: I state my case, then you reply; and when I'm tired of it, I'll just delete or file it.

Our country is living out one of the greatest oxymorons of all time: the problem with our country is drugs, and the problem with our country is not enough drugs. As we continue to fight the war on drugs on our streets, we continue to prescribe drugs for people who lack the ability to fix their attention on anything for any length of time. The most common diagnosis of our children, and young adults is that of Attention Deficit Disorder (ADD), or Attention Deficit Hyperactivity Disorder (ADHD). Whether you have been diagnosed or not, the message is clear: we struggle with wandering minds.

Think about the way we watch television. Al Michaels, longtime sports commentator of ABC, was asked why baseball seems to be dying. He said one thing: remote controls. Years ago we didn't have remotes, so we turned on Saturday's game and there it stayed. But now we can't sit still during the game; we channel surf constantly.[2] With so many options, with cable and satellites, we must scan the channels to see what we might be missing. Commercials used to last one minute, now they last 30 seconds or less. They start loud, fast, and provocative. Everything about them screams "NO, DON'T LEAVE YET!"

Unfortunately that's what we as ministers say every time we take the pulpit. We feel like begging for people's attention. "DON'T TALK; DON'T MAKE OUT YOUR GROCERY LIST; DON'T EVEN THINK ABOUT LUNCH!" We complain that people aren't deep enough and that's why they won't pay attention to our waxing eloquently about doctrine and theology. But the truth is that the Bible has set no precedent for boredom. It is full of rich, invigorating, suspenseful, and even sensual material. The problem may not be the text but the presentation. We simply need to understand how to better unfold these amazing truths while walking the fine line of marketing and the mundane.

WHAT EXACTLY ARE WE TRYING TO DO?

John Ortberg, a member of the teaching team at Willow Creek Community Church, posed the question at a preaching seminar, "How do you know if you've preached a good sermon?" He was addressing the issue of what our true mission is when we get behind the pulpit. He listed a variety of possible answers: 1) explain a theological truth you are interested in, 2) champion the hobby horse of a former seminary professor, 3) speak for twenty minutes without people getting fidgety, or 4) evoke a variety of emotions: applause, tears, laughter. After circling the issue for a time, he brought the topic back to this passage from Mark 1:14-15: "After John was put in prison, Jesus went into Galilee, proclaiming the good news of God. 'The time has come,' he said. 'The kingdom of God is near. Repent and believe the good news!'" Jesus stated what was coming, and then he told them how to get ready. In short, Jesus was interested in changing hearts with the good news. He was interested in spiritual formation. We can easily be persuaded off the course we need to take to fulfill our true mission.[3]

EXIT RAMPS WE SOMETIMES TAKE
⬦ "Wow . . . This Guy Is Deep!"

One barometer we often use to measure our homoletical worth is that of wonder. I serve in a church that is just a few miles away from a seminary, and we have several professors and students that attend. I find it very tempting to prepare sermons with them in mind: "What will blow their minds?" "What will really show them I'm on their level?" In fact, some of the students are so used to being in the world of academia that they offer soothing criti- cism of "I really need something deeper." As a preacher trying to connect with an unchurched postmod- ern mind, I can't be steered in this direction. Just as much as it is not our place to water down the text for easy consumption, it is also not our mission to intellectually impress. The mission is to connect so that spiritual formation can begin.

Our mission is to connect, not to intellectually impress.

"Wow . . . This Guy Is Funny!"

Another way we leave the pulpit feeling confident is when we hear the ringing of laughter in our ears. We complete our monologue of the best material we've got and walk off shouting, "Thank you very much! I'll be here all week!" This one is an easy tempter as well.

Humor can be a great way to connect. I had a professor once say, "If you can get them to lean their head back in laughter, it is then easier to slit their throat with conviction." I certainly agree with this, but it can be overdone and then can become self-serving. I struggle with this because I love to laugh and see others laugh. I have to constantly ask myself, "Will this enhance or distract from my point?" "Does this even have a point?"

Just as much as these questions are valid for humor, they are valid for evoking any type of emotion. In a world of inauthenticity we don't want to be accused of trying to manipulate with any form of emotionalism, whether it is a funny story about your kids in the grocery store, or a tearjerker about a dog saving a family from a fire. Once again, it is our mission to connect and allow spiritual formation to begin.

Staying on Course in an Effective Manner

I think we all agree about the goal of spiritual formation. It is an amazing thing to see a heart that has been callused for years from either decadent behavior or legalistic chains to allow the Holy Spirit to overtake him and begin forming in him a new life. The question in this age of postmodernity is how do we best set this in motion?

Recently I received a call from a woman who was distraught about the elements we use to help people connect such as music, video, and drama. I tried to reason with her about the methods that Jesus used. He used common stories about sheep, coins, and lost sons. He used object lessons of bread, wine, mud, and water.[4] He clearly modeled for us a way to connect with people through the means of the ordinary and contemporary. Her response was, "Well, he wouldn't do that if he lived today."

I'm not sure if she doesn't speak for many of our ministries. We expect people to learn our language, customs, and secret handshakes and then we will introduce them to Jesus. Jesus seemed to be more interested in using whatever it took to make sure that anyone could understand. So what are some ways that we can build a bridge to these new-culture dwellers that have tolerance in their hearts, skepticism in their heads, and remote controls in their hands?

> We expect people to learn our language, customs, and secret handshakes.

Begin Communicating When They Walk in the Door[5]

Have you ever noticed how your surroundings influence your behavior? Certain places or friends just evoke different emotions. Take eating for instance. If you go into a restaurant and see cloth napkins, candlelit tables, and seven forks by your plate, your level of anticipation and investment intensifies. You expect to both give and receive a great amount. But, if you are eating at a picnic, suddenly your expectations change. People will eat anything when they are outside—frozen burgers, spoiled potato salad, hot dogs off the ground. It's almost as if we think we just crashed the plane fifty yards back and we are struggling for survival. We expect little and we give little.

In a similar fashion, we tell people what to expect when they enter our building. If it is cold and silent with old bulletins in the pews and outdated flyers on the walls, we are telling people not to expect much. But if there is a sense of energy, a look of preparation, a visually engaging stage, suddenly people are anticipating something.

Our message begins when people enter the building, so what is the message we want to send. Ravi Zacharias states that postmodern people "think with their hearts, and listen with their eyes."[6] If the goal is reflection, then dim the lights, light some candles around the room, and play soft background music before the service begins. If the goal is energy, then use some colored lights, play some upbeat and contemporary music, and utilize the stage with message-enhancing object lessons.

When people enter the building, they will begin to look around at the people and the décor. There is a fine line when it comes to greeters. You want people who are more than bulletin holders, but you don't want them to be overbearing. Many who attend will want to remain anonymous yet know they are welcome. So choose people who can communicate more than "Hi" yet know when to leave the person alone. The visitor needs to know that she is wanted, hasn't broken any secret codes, and knows who to ask if she has any questions. One church has this motto, "Everybody gets a look, a word, and a touch."[7]

As far as decor goes, allowing the artists in your community to display their work, especially when it ties in to the sermon, will invest value into them and engage the hearts of other artists who aren't yet involved. A church in Denver uses their facility to host community art exhibits, poetry readings, and short film showings. The result has been hundreds of connections and relationships with unchurched artistic people who now feel accepted by the church.[8] Weekly, your church has the opportunity to project either a message of focused energy and intentional direction or one of "this is the way we always do it."

Let's talk about worship for a moment. We are beginning to notice that the songs that precede our message have a profound impact on how prepared people are for the subject matter. The recent consideration in many churches has been the word "thematic." It is a valid point to say that the songs should tie into the message that is being delivered. If the minister is to speak on grieving the loss of a loved one, it is not beneficial for the song service preceding his message to be to the tune of "Oh, Happy Day." I think we'd all agree that happiness can come from sorrow in the salvation of Jesus, but getting people to resonate with the particular message has to begin by getting them to think about this topic even during the worship time.

> **Rather than all elements tying together, they just need to be heading in the same direction.**

Postmodern worship slightly differs from this approach. Rather than people wanting everything to tie together, they just want everything to move in the same direction. In other words, people today are more likely to ask, "Are we moving in some direction," rather than, "What is the theme?" It's the difference between driving to New York or everyone just wearing Yankees hats in the car driving anywhere.

The goal of the worship leader is to be the lead worshiper, the bus driver, so to speak, that leads everyone to a point where the message can reach the fertile soil of a tilled heart. Postmodern worship leaders Chris Tomlin and Louie Giglio, detailed it this way at a worship conference. They said there are basically four moves that a worship experience can make. First, to man about man: songs that are sung by the people about the people. For instance a lyric like "Lean on Me." Second, to man about God: songs that are sung by the people to God. For instance a lyric like "We Need Jesus." Third, to God about man: songs sung to God about our human condition. For example, "We Need You, Lord." Finally, songs that are very personal to God: to God about God. This can be seen in a lyric such as "You Are Holy." These types of transitions are more focused than just moving from fast songs to slow songs, or picking songs based on fluid key changes. They require us to move our people to a central focus. The destination may change based upon the message, which is why it is key that the worship leader and the preacher have detailed dialogue on a weekly basis. If the message truly begins before the sermon, then every person involved in the service needs to understand the final destination.[9]

The Sermon Introduction Needs to Back Up a Few Paces

What about the sermon itself? How can we even begin to try to grab the attention of this hyperactive world? Years ago the most engaging way to begin a sermon was to simply define what we were talking about. Many ministers took the pulpit, gazed into their congregation's eyes, and proclaimed these thought-provoking words: "*Webster's Dictionary* defines 'Patience' as . . .". From here the minister would begin his proclamation of "ought, should, and must" regarding this absolute. We attempt to get people interested in what Paul is saying by telling some stories, maybe a joke, or perhaps reading a poem. The trouble with this approach for the postmodern mind isn't that it doesn't engage, it's that nothing is at stake. No one ever channel surfs, stops at the Discovery Channel, and says "Hey, I was wondering about the nesting patterns of the Meadowlark!" But people do stop on the Home and Garden Channel if Bob Villa is fixing a leaking faucet and the viewer can hear his own dripping in the kitchen. The question many will ask as they listen is not, "What is Paul saying in this text?" but rather, "Why should I keep listening?"

For example, 1 Corinthians 13 is a beautiful example of what love truly is. There is great imagery of clanging gongs and noisy cymbals. Paul uses these images to let us know how awkward and obnoxious life can be without love. It is tempting for the minister to see Paul's illustrations and simply illustrate them again. We could begin with a funny story about being obnoxious, or a ringing alarm clock, or even a nagging boss. But all that does is illustrate an illustration; it does not engage the audience to desire to engage the text. These kinds of illustrations can be used throughout the message, but as a means for introduction, they will fall flat.

The real question people are asking is not what does bad love look like, but what is lost if I don't ever learn how to love. Setting up the text with stories of broken marriages, struggles in your own life with failing to love at all costs, and the desolate nature we all discover when we constantly pursue ourselves rather than sacrificial love would cause an audience to lean in with pencil in hand. Everyone wants to know how to overcome these potential relationship pitfalls. When preparing the introduction, a minister would do well to always ask the question, "Why would anyone want to keep listening?" This does not mean that we manufacture false hope and "how-tos" that reduce the message down to a cheap cliché, but rather that we direct their attention to the true life-changing hope that Jesus brings in all areas of our lives. After all, everyone wants a better workplace, a better home, a better future, and a better heart. With these as the destination even the more difficult subjects of surrender, sacrifice, and tithing can find welcome ears.

The Body of the Sermon Should Be Communicated with Variety

We are often guilty of training our people in what to expect. For those of us who use the same style of outlines, we can watch as our people begin to put their notes away and reach for their coats once we get to the third point. This is one of the difficulties of putting fill-in-the-blank outlines in the bulletin. It's great for giving out information, but as soon as that last blank is filled, you can almost hear the rattle of car keys. Here is a listing of methods that help break up monotony and increase variety at communicating the message.

1. Scripture Telling

Eugene Peterson in his paraphrase of the Bible, *The Message*, highlights for us the need to put things in modern language. Sometimes rather than just reading the text, especially if it is a narrative passage to begin with, the preacher would connect better by telling it in a modern setting. People don't necessarily immediately connect with the magnitude of the problem of a son who took his inheritance and ran away from home, but they do know the tension of a son who says, "Dad, I wish you were dead, and I'm leaving home to pursue an alternative lifestyle." Telling these stories will set you up better to read the real text later in the message.

2. Personal Stories

Everyone in a postmodern congregation wants to know how the teacher wrestles with the things we teach. To be so honest as to say, "Let me tell you how I struggle with the problem outlined in this passage" goes a long way in letting people know that we are all on this journey together. In this culture the minister isn't looked upon as having to be perfect, just real.

I can recall preaching a sermon on worry. Halfway through the message I read the text from Matthew 6, stepped closer to the audience and said, "Can I be honest with you? I don't like this passage. I am a habitual worrier." I then began telling stories of my personal struggles with anxiety. Suddenly everyone leaned in with a look of "I'm glad I'm not the only one!" Another time I preached on healing. I wrestled with all of the theological ramifications of whether or not God heals today, is it contingent on faith, or is it based on how many times I ask. I presented all of these truths, and then I told a personal struggle I've had in dealing with diabetes. I mentioned that people had prayed for me before to be healed, but it never happened. I simply had to understand that God is still in control even if he doesn't fix all of my problems. I had more response from people regarding that story than I did any other point I made. People want to know that we have the same questions they do, yet we still find faith in the sovereignty of God.

3. Metaphors

One of the biggest television hits of our time was the real-life experiences of sixteen people stranded on a desert island. *Survivor* consumed the television viewing time of many postmodern people. It's as if we became tired with staged drama and we scratched an itch with real-life drama. Each week we would watch as someone would be voted off the island by his or her teammates. One of the more interesting things about the show was the number of symbols they used. A person didn't just win a competition; he also got to wear a special necklace. A team didn't just win a game; they got to hold a trophy until the next competition. And when someone was voted off the island, she had to have her tiki torch extinguished to symbolize her life being snuffed out on the island. Did we really need these things? Wouldn't we know what was going on without having symbols? The fact is that our culture loves to attach emotional significance to physical objects.

This serves the church well because we have many symbols with great significance. Baptism and communion should now be a place for more interaction, more explanation, and more focus given. Let a person share his testimony from the baptistery. If he's too shy, have someone read it as he enters the water, or show a prerecorded video of him telling his story. Allow communion to be interactive by placing stations around the room. Explain what the emblems mean, give the people time to prayerfully walk to the tables around the room, and display pictures of Jesus on the wall through physical art or Power Point presentation.

As for preaching, dare I say that youth ministers could teach us a thing or two? Object lessons allow people to infuse spiritual truths onto physical objects. Use visual words to carry your outline: "a road we travel, a suitcase we all carry, a blueprint we all need, or obstacles we all face." One service we handed out puzzle pieces to everyone who entered the room. The subject we discussed was the missing pieces to your life and how Jesus could meet those needs. At the end, people were encouraged to surrender at the communion tables their puzzle pieces, allowing them to symbolize the emptiness in life. This proved to be a very moving metaphor.

4. Build Tension

One of the ways many of us have preached is to "sweep the floor" of the subject. We begin with a question, and then allow "It's not this, not this, but this" to serve as our outline. For instance: What does it take to get to heaven? It's not works, it's not family, it's not wealth—it's Jesus. This is a great way to build constant tension while maintaining the attention of your audience as they begin to wonder as well. This technique is one of the most helpful I've seen. It causes people to constantly ask questions that you can then answer for them.

One way to increase the tension is to say things they think but would never expect to hear in church. A message that makes this bold statement at the beginning: "I wonder where God is when it hurts!" or "If God is so good, then why is there so much evil in the world?" or "Surely all roads and religions lead to God!" These will cause an audience to wonder where in the world you are going and at the same time beg to go with you.[10]

5. Audience Participation

If you want to really step out on a limb, try to get the audience involved in more ways than just listening. Try having a question and answer time at the end of your message. Ask people to write down their questions and hand them to you at the end of the sermon (or e-mail them to you), and then take time to address them next week (anonymously of course). Make comments to your audience like: "Have you ever felt like this? Let's see a show of hands" or "What's your least favorite holiday? Talk about it with the people next to you." Then ask them to tell you what they think right there during your message.

One way to really mix things up is to let the audience choose what they want to hear. It is possible with some topics to have a variety of texts and directions to go. Try starting the message going one direction, stop and give them two choices to vote on as to where we go from here, and then, based on the vote, take the next avenue for that message. This requires preparing around three different messages for one service. Enjoy!

Illustrations in Many Shapes and Sizes

One of the great struggles of the minister's week is trying to find illustrations that engage the audience and bring insight into the text. The temptation is to reduce the illustrative time down to a canned story from a book of illustrations that we found in the Christian bookstore. While it is true that many of these stories produce awe, wonder, laughter, or even tears, they often fail to communicate reality and authenticity. The real-life stories that a minister delivers always cause an audience to lean in instead of back. One practice that may help is committing to the writing out of one person- al story each day. It doesn't have to be lengthy or profound, but the discipline will force you to be watching for things to write about and subsequently share.

> In this postmodern world, variety is welcomed.

Fortunately in this postmodern world, variety is welcomed. This may seem like an added stress, but actually it increases our resources for illustrations that connect. The aforementioned object lessons can carry a message all the way through. People are interested in what it is you hold in your hand, or point to on stage. This creates a vehicle for communication.

One mechanism that connects well is a testimony. Allowing someone from the congregation to tell his story will validate your message and give value to the one who shares. Some tips on testimonies: have people submit a written copy of what they plan to say so you can make sure it fits. Make sure you stress the need to communicate what God is doing in their life, or what life is like now that they have come to Christ. The last thing you want is for the sermon to become a soapbox for someone to express his or her political views or moment of conversion during an episode of *One Life to Live*.

Another effective mechanism of illustrative material is the use of multimedia. This comes in many forms: a video clip from a movie or television show will resonate with this culture enamored with entertainment, and so will using a song from the radio to highlight the questions we are all asking. Oftentimes the church is fearful of using forms of media that are considered secular, but the truth is that culture and its entertainment are windows into the soul of lost people. Using tasteful songs or video clips only help connect wondering minds and will later serve as free advertising the next time they encounter that song or movie.

One last technique to hold attention is to split the message up. Preach the first part of the sermon, take a break by using a video clip, special music, or both, and then return to complete the message. Though this requires more attention to detail, it will require less attention to illustrations. This allows people a change in scenery that will reengage their minds. Since the two blocks of time you are speaking are relatively shorter than usual, you will be able to have their attention the entire time.

Conclusion Calls for Action and Response, but Maybe Not "Altar Calls"

Bill Easum once compared the conversion experiences of the modern world to that of the postmodern world. He said the former have Damascus Road experiences, while the latter walk more of an Emmaus Road. The previous generations could hear the truth, be reminded of the righteous life they were called to, and walk the other way. But people who have grown up without God often have to walk with Jesus for awhile before realizing what communing with him really entails.[11] Because of this, the "altar call" or invitation that many of us are used to is becoming a method that is viewed as emotional manipulation. People want to process what they've heard, ask some questions, try some things out, and then in the presence of friends confess Christ and be buried in baptism.

Services that provide moments for interaction through group decision time often begin to teach people what it means to make a commitment to Christ.

Along with asking people to leave their seats and move towards communion, we also use times of prayer altars, candle lighting, and incense burning. It is true that incense got a bad name in the '60s, but the truth is incense has biblical significance. At one service we provided the metaphor of our lives being clay in the hands of God. We had a woman throwing clay pots on a pottery wheel, projected verses about God shaping our lives on the screens, and welcomed people to the front to burn sticks of incense as a sin offering and symbol of prayer to God. It gave us a great opportunity to explain the Old Testament use of incense, and to encourage our participation in this type of sacrifice. As odd as this method seems, our people are deeply moved as they stand and sing songs while pillars of burning incense lift up to God.

At the conclusion of one of our services, I approached the incense table and found a package of cigarettes that someone had surrendered. At another, many witnessed a group of friends leading another friend to Christ. The power of symbols coupled with an opportunity to engage the heart of God provides this experiential culture a more meaningful path to conversion than singing a few more verses of "I Have Decided to Follow Jesus."

> **For this experiential culture there are more meaningful paths.**

Let me conclude by bringing us back to the original question: Do we know this audience we are trying to connect with? Several weeks ago my wife and I were searching for a Rolodex. Nothing fancy, just a cheap paper and plastic device to get phone numbers quickly. We went into an office supply store, located the proper aisle, and proceeded to survey the vast selection. Finally we decided on one, approached the counter. The word "Rolodex," and its color, were listed in three different languages. This company was passionate about connecting with a variety of cultures. They wanted everyone to know about their product. I wonder if we have the same passion?

[1] Leonard Sweet, *Postmodernity Lecture*.

[2] Al Michaels as heard on *The Tony Kornheiser Show*, ESPN Radio, 2000.

[3] John Ortberg, "Preaching that Connects," Audio tape, Leadership Summit, 2000.

[4] Luke 15; John 3; Mark 8.

[5] See Darren Walter, *The People-Magnet Church* (Joplin, MO: College Press, 2001).

[6] Ravi Zacharias, "One Week in October," Audio tape, *Apologetics and the Postmodern Mind*. Oxford, 1999.

[7] Frontline Ministry, McLean Bible Church. McLean, VA.

[8] The Next Level Church. Wheat Ridge, CO.

[9] Louie Giglio and Chris Tomlin, *Postmodern Worship*, Worship Together Conference, Nashville, October 2000.

[10] This type of tension building in preaching is explored and detailed in the writings and teachings of Eugene Lowry and Fred B. Craddock.

[11] Bill Easum, "Growing Spiritual Redwoods," Audio tape (Wilmore, KY: Beason Institute, 1999).

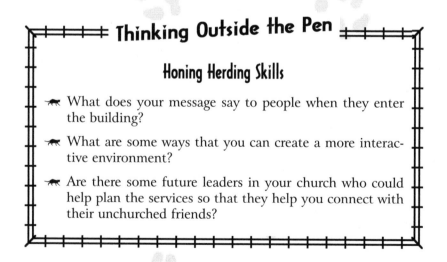

Thinking Outside the Pen

Honing Herding Skills

- What does your message say to people when they enter the building?

- What are some ways that you can create a more interactive environment?

- Are there some future leaders in your church who could help plan the services so that they help you connect with their unchurched friends?

It Worked Yesterday, Why Won't It Work Today?

5

Cats are unpredictable! One day they want you to pet them, maybe even rub their fur the wrong way. But don't try it two days in a row! They can be moody and touchy, or extremely affectionate and comforting. What may have been purrfect one day is peccant the next. You can count sheep, but you can't count on cats! Leading the church in the postmodern world will have such ups and downs, contradictions and surprises. Are we ready for unreadiness?

Growing up, I [Jeff] remember my Dad always working on our cars: oil changes, tune-ups, and pretty much any maintenance that needed to be done on the vehicles. We rarely, if ever, took our cars to the mechanic. Once I was old enough to drive, I had a car. Not a new car, but one that was much more complicated than the cars my father had always owned. One day I noticed some trouble in the engine and asked dad to take a look. I remember him opening up the hood, poking around briefly, and then driving to the local mechanic to have it checked out. He explained to me that cars have changed so much in such a short time, that he couldn't even do simple maintenance anymore. He couldn't even recognize where major parts of the car were.

There are ministers in churches all over the country who are looking under the hood of their churches and scratching their heads. At one time they were experts in church maintenance and ministry, but now, almost overnight, it seems as though the church has changed. Many times, their tendency is to blame themselves, to become discouraged by their inability to "fix the car." It isn't so much the fault of churches or of ministers, but it is just a reality of life. Things change.

David Bowie sang about it, we all know it is a part of life, but why is it so hard to change? Change is the one inevitable aspect of our lives that we cannot escape and that we many times resist. There are times when we even loathe the possibility that something that has always been may not be anymore.

GROWTH BRINGS CHANGE

The first major change in my life came when I was in kindergarten and had to make the "big move" to first grade. I remember my mother preparing me for the changes that would occur the following spring. She explained that she would no longer drop me off or pick me up from school, but that from now on I would ride the bus. Despite her desire to convince me of the good aspects of this change, I couldn't help but detect the fear in her voice. She was afraid for her little boy and the fact that he would have to ride the bus with the "big kids." I was equally fearful of the same issues. She told me riding a bus meant I was growing up and becoming a young man, and I explained to her that I didn't give a rip about growing up, I wanted her to take me to school.

She also explained to me that I wouldn't be having snack time anymore, and that I would be eating my lunch at school. She told how instead of going to the library for story time, I would be learning how to read on my own. All of those things that Mom was using to convince of the value of first grade squelched my desire to go. But I went, and what I found surprised me. The bus ride was fun. There were a lot of other kids just like me, and we had a good time. Learning to read meant that I was no longer at the mercy of the story reader in the library and her choice of books, but now I was able to read things that were of interest to me.

Those changes weren't as bad as I thought, but that isn't what made first grade so impressive. What made me like first grade more than anything were the things that I discovered in my change that my mother didn't even tell me about. Instead of snack time, we had recess. Recess was a brilliant idea. Another hidden pearl in first grade was gym class. Structured recess! Even more brilliant than plain old recess, and I almost passed out every time our gym teacher would break out the parachute. The benefits of first grade certainly were strong enough to pacify any fears I might have had with the change. Fortunately, someone was looking out for me. She knew what I needed and forced change even when I wasn't willing to on my own. Because of that, I was able to grow up and become a well-equipped and semi-adjusted citizen. Had I been given the choice, though, I would still be sitting on a carpet square, listening to stories and waiting in line at the door for Mom to pick me up. Change is inevitable, and we can choose to embrace it or stick our heads in the sand and let the world pass us by. Those are the options.

Our options are to embrace change or stick our heads in the sand.

Our church has been given the opportunity to start a satellite ministry to postmoderns in the arts community of our city. The building we are using was an old Baptist congregation founded in 1946. When the church was in its heyday, it was one of the larger churches in our city, but eventually their ability to effectively minister to their community was lost. The city had dramatically changed, and they remained the same. They were wonderful Christian men and women (the fifteen who were left of a congregation of 600 at one time). The day we met to change the ownership of the property (they gave it to us, which will be a story for another book), I could see the sadness in their eyes. They knew that they had missed a huge opportunity to preach the word of God, but because of their unwillingness or inability to change they were now closing the doors.

Nowhere is it more difficult for change to be embraced than in the church. The church is the place where things are always the same. We can grow up in a church, become so used to its cadence and rhythm, and then go away for years or even decades, and then in many cases walk back in the doors on any given Sunday and be in step, like we never left. We will know what song will be sung after the offering, that if it is the third Sunday, a potluck lunch will follow. We know that we stand during the last verse of the closing song, and we know that nothing has changed.

> The church has been the one place where things always stayed the same.

Down the road, in the little town where the church resides, there is nothing but change. At the gas stations, the pumps now accept credit cards, and you can watch television when you pump your gas. In the grocery store you no longer have to wait in line for a cashier, you can check yourself out. You don't even need to go into the convenience store any-more, you can do all of your shopping on your home com-puter and have the products delivered to your door. The world is in a perpetual state of change, and yet, when you walk into the church, it's as if the members haven't been outside of their doors in years. Yet church leaders stand at the door looking out into a strange land and ask themselves, "It worked yesterday, why won't it work today?"

The inevitability of change is a part of the fabric of life. We know it must happen, and yet we never want it to happen. There are three ways that we can handle change. First, we can bury our heads in the proverbial sand and try to ignore changes in our culture and in our communities. Many churches and leaders choose to do this. If I ignore it, maybe it will go away and leave me alone. The second common method in handling change is to fight against it. Those women who write nasty anonymous notes week after week asking if the organ is broken are fighting change. But it isn't only they. Leaders of churches will fight in committee meetings to hold on to the "sacred traditions" of the church rather than to consider changing them. I believe the healthy way to deal with change is not only to just accept it, but also to anticipate it and embrace it. Leadership not only tells the troops where to go, but also it scouts ahead and does strategic planning. The church that understands and embraces the need for change will be a church that effectively is able to communicate the gospel to emerging cultures.

> The healthy way to deal with change is to anticipate it and embrace it.

RESISTANT TO CHANGE

Who is my neighbor? The Pharisees asked this question of Jesus, and we would do well to ask it of ourselves. If the summation of the law and the prophets rest on the truth of loving God and loving our neighbors, then we had better begin to understand our neighbors.

I was driving to a wedding in rural USA. I hadn't passed a car, a gas station, or a restaurant in an hour and I was fifteen miles from a town with a stoplight. As I turned the corner, I saw an enormous neon sign above the trees. It was for a church. I immediately slowed down, thinking I must have stumbled upon the Christian Mecca of the farm belt, and as I arrived at the building, I saw a small country church with a gravel parking lot. A sign salesman had certainly done a good job in convincing this congregation that neon signs call people to the Lord, and he also probably made a good commission.

There is nothing wrong with little country churches in rural America; in fact, we desperately need those congregations, but I wonder how valuable the neon is? The church must constantly evaluate her surroundings and audience in order to make sure that she is effectively communicating the gospel. The church must implement useful change in the marketplace in order to embrace the changing world in which she finds herself. Incredibly that world is changing faster each day.

Why is it so hard for the church to embrace the doctrine of change? On some level I believe we have set ourselves up for this situation. Most church leaders would never say that they are opposed to change. They would never say that they purposely program against change or that they have figured out what church is supposed to look like. But many operate their churches with those preconceptions in mind. They believe that the church is a reality to be achieved, an end to a means. That all we need to do is to have the right complementary ingredients and then maintain the organization. Problems in the church are simply a matter of missing ingredients! We search for a new adult education minister, or a new children's minister who can come in and supply the missing ingredient. All the while we are missing the point. We don't need to analyze the ingredients so much as we need to assure how we cook the recipe!

There are two main reasons we resist change. The first is because we are *selfish*. We have worked hard at developing a system of religious participation that we feel comfortable with, and we are not about to open its value up for discussion. Our attitude communicates, "If you don't like it, go somewhere else." And the message has been heard loud and clear as Xers and beyond are fleeing mainline Protestant churches at an alarming rate. If we are going to reach the next generations, we must be ready to release the stranglehold of control we have on the church and allow different yet Christ-centered ideas to begin to season our congregations.

The other reason that we resist change is that we are afraid of what *might* happen. We are scared of the unknown and largely uncontrolled possibilities of a church in the hands of twenty-somethings. Yet, when you come right down to it, things *are going* to change. You have already read some concepts about leading and ministering in a postmodern world that I am sure have made you want to forget you had ever heard the word "postmodern." Postmoderns are different from the generations that have preceded them. Because of that, what worked when we walked out of Bible college a few years ago may not work today. In fact, if it worked last year, it may not work today.

Postmoderns are dying for a spiritual connection, not a religious form. They are not interested in the expression of church that we are currently peddling. It would seem that we are *pushing* the rope of Christianity instead of pulling it. It appears from the outside looking in that we are trying desperately to revive and patch together something that may have run its course. We might be better off to take some of our models behind the barn and put them out of their misery. But that's so hard to do, to deviate from the normal way that church is supposed to be done. We must look to our community, the people with whom we have been allowed to minister, and see what it is that will meet their constantly changing needs.

> **Postmoderns are dying for a spiritual connection, not a religious form.**

For some, the movement from using the hymnal to singing choruses would split the church, and I would guess that this scenario has already happened in some churches. It would mean that we would have to scrap all that we know to be true, and in many respects to be holy, and start from scratch.

Postmoderns have grown up knowing nothing but change. Their lives are a study of coping with a world of change: television, computers, the Internet, music, science, travel, and the list could go on. In my lifetime alone I have seen the rise and fall of the vinyl record, eight-track, cassette tape, CD, and now digital music. I have seen beta, VHS, laser disc, cable, digital cable, and DVD. Each one promising so much more than the one before and lasting such a short time.

Comfort in the church used to be found in the familiar. Growing up, no matter what was going on in my life or in the world, one thing I knew I could count on was the church's schedule. I knew and took some comfort in the fact that each week, no matter what else was going on in the world, you could expect the same thing from the church: Sunday morning worship, Sunday night prayer, Wednesday night Bible study, and the third Thursday pitch-in dinners. All of this brought a sense of normalcy to a somewhat disjointed and out-of-control world. It didn't necessarily engage me, but it certainly spoke the language that my parents were speaking, and so we were there every week participating in the scheduled religious activities. In looking back, it seemed as though the system of religion became almost as important as the God whom the system was designed to engage. In fact, many times, *participation* in the system was more important than the *result* of that participation. The minister called people when attendance was falling, yet there were many people in the pews each week whose lives were out of control, who never received a call.

I am sure that when our forefathers developed the "way" church was supposed to be done, they had the best of intentions. I am sure the system was not a system in its original intent, but somewhere, at some time, someone began to value the system a little too highly. We began to defend the "traditions" of the faith at all costs, many times not knowing ourselves from whence those traditions came. We only knew that this was the "way" that we needed to do church. It is time for a change. If we are going to engage the twenty-first-century world with the first-century message of salvation through Jesus Christ alone, then we need to be ready to change.

Many postmoderns are familiar with the church or believe they know enough about the institutional church to decide it is not for them. They have been dragged down the halls of their grandparents' church on holidays and special occasions. They have been thrown into a crowded classroom wearing their Sunday best that barely fit last year. They have sat through long, boring sermons, listened to outdated music played on boring instruments, and they have had enough. But they still need Jesus. They still long to express themselves spiritually and unfortunately are doing just that in all kinds of places with all kinds of people, but rarely in a church of Jesus Christ. Religious literature of all kinds accounted for a record percentage of sales last year and it is expected to increase over the next five years. People are hungry, but they think our food is spoiled!

> The notable thing about the first-century church is that they were starting from scratch.

We talk a lot about the first-century church as if they had it all figured out. It wasn't so much that the first-century church was the perfect example (as the Corinthian church demonstrates) as much as they were starting from scratch. The call to follow Jesus was radical. Not only was the call to follow

Jesus radical, but also the form in which people engaged God was completely different. The Jews were forced to change the way they worshiped God or be left behind in the wake of the Holy Spirit's movement.

THE CHURCH: NEW FORMS AND FRESH EXPRESSIONS

One of the temptations will be to take our systematic modern mind-set and simply insert postmodern methods. The sin in this would be in our canonizing these structures and viewing them as infallible. Just because we learn of an effective method in the Northeast, doesn't mean that the same method will work in the Midwest. There are certainly things we can learn, and elements we can implement, but seeing this as a cookie-cutter formula will lead us into idolizing the new systems. If change is something that took place every forty years in previous generations, we may find that change must happen every two years in the postmodern world. Because the methods we use will quickly become outdated and ineffective, our goal must be to discover what values must be held despite our chosen relevant method.

The first place we could start would be with our definition of church. Many times our problems in life come from an inability to define the problem. I drive a Ford Tempo. Not the most flashy of cars, but reliable and relatively easy for me to work on. One day, I went out to start my car. I placed the key in the ignition, turned it, and I did not hear a sound. I wasn't going anywhere. Now I am not a mechanic, but I do consider myself somewhat intelligent. Though I couldn't discuss the finer details of internal combustion, I do know the basics. I immediately diagnosed the problem and set out to the auto parts store to get the right parts. I stood at the counter and asked the gentleman for the part I needed, a starter. He found it and quickly sent me on my way. Now, during this entire process, I was feeling rather proud of myself for taking on such a project. In fact I began thinking of the other projects around the house that I could knock out after I finished installing this new starter.

I arrived home ready to tackle the project. Two hours later, I was under the car, still trying to determine which bolts needed to be removed in order to get the old starter out. I was frustrated, tired, ready to give up, and not feeling entirely ministerial. But I would not be deterred. This car was getting a new starter whether it needed it or not. Four hours and many prayers later, I had finally installed the new starter and was ready to try it out. Fortunately, my father-in-law had just arrived from out of town for the weekend and he would be there to witness what a wonderful and resourceful man his daughter had married. I explained to him that the car wouldn't start and I had diagnosed the problem as a faulty starter. I jumped in the car, turned the key and felt the weight of the world drop right on top of my head. Still nothing. Five hours after I had begun this quick project, I was back where I started. My father-in-law, a very mechanical man, slid under the car and checked my connections and told me to try it again. I did with the same result. He slid out from under the car and asked a simple question that will haunt me until the day I go to the grave. It is a question that has exposed me for what I truly am, mechanically inept. He asked, "Did you check the battery first?" I wanted to say yes, but I had to say no. I hadn't even thought twice about the battery. The most visible electrical piece of equipment under the hood of my car, and I hadn't even considered that it might be the problem.

My father-in-law attacked the problem. In ten minutes we had the battery out of the car. In twenty we were at the parts store having it tested. In twenty-five minutes I was again coming face-to-face with my ignorance. The man who sold me the starter also sold me the battery and with a grin quipped, "Come and see us again!" Inside of an hour, my car was running like a fine-tuned machine. I take solace only in the fact that though my original starter was fine, I did correct-ly install the new one.

I spent valuable time, money, and energy trying to fix some-thing that didn't need to be fixed because I had not taken the time to correctly diagnose the prob-lem. I believe many churches have real-ized that something needs to be done in their congregation and are going to great lengths to identify and fix things that may not be broken, all the while missing the real problem directly under their noses.

> I believe many churches miss the real problem directly under their noses.

We don't need to redefine what the church is, but we do need to rethink the form in which the first-century church is lived in the twenty-first-century culture. Sometimes our defi-nitions are right, but our application of those definitions is wrong. Sometimes our intentions are good, but our strategy is bad. Some of our problems in engaging the postmodern world are found in our congregational forms. Forms tell a lot about the values of the congregation.

Many congregations look around their pews on Sunday morning and scratch their heads and wonder why there aren't more young people in the church. What they fail to recognize is that the form that their church has taken appeals primarily to those people who are there, to the generations that have come before. They do not appeal to the generations that are now emerging.

The form that most churches choose to accomplish their mission is centered on the large group celebration. We call this "worship." The church is expressive when the people gather to listen to the music, fellowship with their friends, and hear the preacher. There is very little, if any, individual par-ticipation in the traditional church.

Since our corporate gatherings aren't attracting postmoderns, the first thing we try to solve the problem is to dress our current structure in different clothes, hoping that a facelift will attract the people we think we are looking for. We find someone to play the guitar, and we sing some choruses. Nothing happens. We try again and this time we wear a flannel shirt, light candles, and serve coffee. Still nothing. We have tried to spice up the ingredients, but we haven't taken a good hard look at the recipe. If we are going to engage emerging generations, the form of our church will have to embrace what is valuable to them. Postmoderns value relationships. They thrive on relationships. They long to interact and socialize and connect relationally with other people.

Think about that for a moment and then evaluate your church. Think of the one place where you expect all people who are "involved" in your church to be on a weekly basis. The one place that you consider to be the true expression of your church. If your church is like most churches, you would identify your Sunday morning worship service as the place. Now consider the values of postmoderns. Will the need of the person you are trying to reach ever be met through the method of ministry you are employing? No matter what kind of music you play, no matter how casual you dress when you preach, no matter how many pop video clips you show, no matter what time the service starts, if people cannot connect in relationships, they will not connect with you. If the most important aspect of your church does not meet the most pressing need of the people, then both will suffer. The church will not grow, and people will not hear or see the Word of God. Our methods for reaching postmoderns must engage their value system.

> **If people cannot connect in relationships, they will not connect with you.**

We are talking about community, and there are many ways to go about meeting this need practically for relational connection and to develop a sense of authentic, Christ-centered community. As postmoderns make relational connections, in a Christ-centered atmosphere, life change occurs. We need to provide those opportunities.

For some churches, this might take the form of an alternative weekly worship setting. Many churches are taking this type of approach. They are starting new services, at alternative times, with relationships as the focus. When you walk into one of these services, the setting resembles a coffeehouse or a club atmosphere. Round tables and chairs are spread out around the room, encouraging people to interact with one another. During the service, there might be questions that the congregation is asked to answer. Sometimes weekly worship might not even include the traditional "sermon." Some churches, like Apex in Las Vegas and Common Ground in Indianapolis, are taking the emphasis off the large, corporate celebration. They are moving to a "house church" model where people engage one another in biblical study, worship, prayer, service, and communion. In these house churches people are able to make relational connections in a Christ-centered community.

Whatever our congregation looks like, it is time for a change. Though it will not be easy (change never is) the process will probably teach us a lot more about who God is than the change itself.

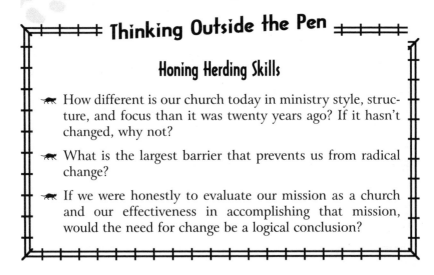

Thinking Outside the Pen

Honing Herding Skills

- 🐾 How different is our church today in ministry style, structure, and focus than it was twenty years ago? If it hasn't changed, why not?

- 🐾 What is the largest barrier that prevents us from radical change?

- 🐾 If we were honestly to evaluate our mission as a church and our effectiveness in accomplishing that mission, would the need for change be a logical conclusion?

Everyone to the Rainbow Deck for Shuffleboard!

6

"Cats, can't live with them, can't shoot 'em," according to an anonymous dog lover. Lazy, apathetic, cool, unconcerned, bratty, inattentive . . . how do you herd such cats? How can you plan enough variety to cater to such animals? Did someone say, "Chill"? Our challenge is to maintain a fluid flexibility.

The plan seemed flawless. What better way to gather people than coffee and karaoke. In my mind, it was a "no lose" situation. I [Jeff] carefully planned the evening, thought of all the details, and prepared for one spectacular outreach opportunity. What I found was that my calling as pastor and my passion to connect people who were not connected to the church didn't include the gift of event planning. Karaoke bombed! In fact, it was so bad that the people I invited told me later that they felt sorry for me but didn't know how to break the news. I was a failure in ministry. I began to question my calling. After all, if I couldn't plan a fun

93

"event," how in the world was I going to make it in the world of young adult and singles ministry? I was doomed. All the books, the conferences, the propaganda on ministering to postmoderns taught that they need to experience the gospel relationally. I assumed that my role was to be the cruise director, the social coordinator. In many ways the church validated my assumption. I was in charge of the social needs of the young adults that went to our church. It got so bad that people were calling me during the week asking me what we were going to do on the weekend. They wanted to know what kind of fun and games I had arranged to meet their social needs. My first two years of young adult ministry were fraught with Super Bowl parties and weekend cookouts that rarely reached any spiritual depth or biblical instruction.

We find ourselves living in a consumer-based, consumption-driven culture. People want as much as they can get with the least amount of effort. Thousands of products and services are developed to make our lives easier and more hassle free. This consumer mentality has made its way into the church and unfortunately the church has responded to meet the demands of her consumer base. In many cases, the church resembles the YMCA, with no membership fee and no minimum stay required. We set up a buffet of programs and services and then allow people to feast. When they tire of our menu, they will tell you they are not being fed anymore, and move on to another buffet that offers a slightly different menu. We are then reduced to improving our buffet and even going to the extent of designing specific menus for hungry people. We find ourselves settling for this model of ministry.

> In many cases the church resembles the YMCA with no membership fee and no minimum stay.

The early church was the opposite of this consumer mentality. In Acts 8, we see the persecution of the church leading to the scattering of the Christians in Jerusalem to Judea and Samaria. The interesting part of this dispersion is that the apostles stayed in Jerusalem. This church, which had once been led by the apostles, was transformed into a church that had equipped Christians to fill the role the apostles had filled. Stephen went from being one who aided in the food distribution to the widows, to one who preached boldly in the Synagogue of the Freedmen and died for his faith. Philip, one who also was a part of the seven, went to Samaria and proclaimed the Christ there. The expectation for the Christians in Jerusalem was different than the expectations we have of our congregations.

People will rarely rise above the expectations that we set for them. Early in my ministry, I realized that I had set my expectations too low, and the people I was ministering to were wallowing in those low expectations, wanting nothing more than what I was offering. It would be my guess that had the Christians in Jerusalem been given the opportunity, they would have much rather stayed home, enjoying the teaching of the apostles and the early community life of the church in Jerusalem. The apostles were not interested in providing a buffet of programs, but in equipping people to minister the Word of God as they went into "all the world." It became glaringly obvious that my passion for ministry and the plan that I had to quench that passion were going in two different directions. It was time for a philosophical change.

JOURNEYMEN

The beginning of moving postmoderns to ministry will first require a change in the understanding of the minister's role in the postmodern setting. We often relate to others through a framework they cannot use. Ministers over the years have been seen as the Bible-answer men. They appear to the congregation they serve as the ones with all of the knowledge of Christ, and the lifestyle to match. We know this isn't true, and there isn't a doubt that we would ever proclaim to our congregations that we have arrived (Phil. 3:12). Post-moderns aren't looking for someone who has all the answers even though they have many questions. They are searching for a community of people that are asking the same questions they're asking and for people who are on the same journey.

I received a phone call from a young lady in her twenties who had been married for a little over a year. She and her husband were both believers and were having some serious marital problems. He had just moved out of the house and they needed someone to talk to. She asked if I would be willing to talk with them, and I asked her if they were a part of a congregation already. She said they were, but what she said next really struck me. She said, "We are a part of a church, but we don't want to talk with the minister of that church because we have to see him every week." I knew the church and also knew it was a strong, Bible-teaching congregation. I also knew that if the minister there had known of our conversation, he would have probably been hurt by the expectation that people in his congregation felt they needed to measure up, and if they didn't they had to turn to someone else to help them. I told the young woman that she needed to talk with her minister about the issue first.

In ministering to postmoderns, we first need to begin to journey with them. To let them in on our world through transparency and honesty, letting them know that we are human too, and while we have been called to the ministry of the Word, we still are on a journey as they are to realize our potential in Christ.

Repeatedly I hear the same thing from the people who come to our church. "We really like the fact that we can relate to you." "You are approachable, and we feel like we can talk to you." "You are one of us." They rarely, if ever, comment on the theological depth or the delivery of my messages. They never praise my organizational skills. They like the fact that they know me, that they relate to me, and that they sense we are all in this together. This is not to say that we air our laundry and every struggle of the flesh that we might face, but like Paul, we admit that we too are sinners in need of the grace of God.

> They like the fact that they know me and relate to me.

I find myself caught between two worlds at times, wanting the recognition of being the spiritual giant among "my people" yet also desiring to get out of the way. It is aggravating at times that my ego wants to be stroked. Sometimes I want them to see me as a little more spiritual or holy than they are. Sometimes, I wish they would call me Pastor or Reverend, but instead they just call me Jeff.

One of the many things that I had to change was my understanding of the role of minister. Growing up in church, I assumed the holiest man in the room was the man behind the pulpit. He gave the spiritual instruction, he offered prayers in the language of Moses (which I didn't understand), and he was the man whom everyone wanted to talk to after church and sit next to at the pot luck dinner. He was a spiritual giant among us dwarfed sinners.

I also remember that we had troubles in our churches. I grew up in many different churches and often found that those holy men weren't so holy after all. They were real people, with real temptations and struggles. They had problems with their wives and their children. They struggled with self-esteem and pride and greed and all of the things that the men and women in their pews struggled with each week. The only difference was they weren't allowed to tell anyone. No one wanted to know that their minister was depressed (though if they cared at all, they really knew). The minister certainly didn't want to ruin his image by allowing people to see that he was depressed (though he desperately needed a confidant, a community to share in his struggles with him). So each Sunday morning, he smiled at us and we smiled at him.

Then one day he was gone. Mutually agreeing with the leaders that it would be better if he found a new place to minister. Get a fresh start in a new town to begin the masquerade again. The role of the minister needs to change.

One of the emerging occupations in this new century will be that of "spiritual guide." In the postmodern world, people aren't looking for holy examples in unholy people, but people who are able to journey with them, to help them see and experience the truth of the gospel in everyday circumstances. We must endeavor to be such men and women.

The new age movement is way ahead of us with gurus and spiritualists who are enlisted as guides to help people unlock the "spirit within" and journey with them in the discovery process. I met a very nice woman the other day at a gathering for the youth version of Alcoholics Anonymous. She was the mentor for these young men and women who were dealing with the evil effects of addiction. Every Monday night, she meets with these people to journey through the process of recovery and spiritual exploration. She is a member of a local congregation called the Church Within, a new age church in our city.

After our chat, I began to think about my role as a minister, as a pastor of people who are desperately seeking answers to life's questions, and I felt as though I was missing the boat. It was as if a wave of reality had just crashed down on my head and I knew that if I didn't do something, I would drown in a sea of missed opportunity. My formal training for pastoral ministry did not prepare me for this and my understanding of the role of minister didn't include rolling up my

> My training for pastoral ministry left me ill-eqipped to disciple people.

sleeves and hurting alongside others. I learned how to perform a wedding, how to preach a sermon, and how to schedule meetings, but I was ill equipped to disciple people.

The role of the minister is changing. Not only are the duties themselves changing, but the expectation of the people in our communities is changing as well. In order for us to minister to the postmodern philosophy and the people who live their lives from its foundations, we must be ready to recognize that we are journeymen as well.

FAIRY-TALE FAÇADES

Postmoderns grew up in an era of television evangelism that included preachers who embezzled money from their followers, who committed repeated acts of immorality, and who lied each week to the viewers who tuned in for some "heavenly guidance." They are skeptical of the slick outlines and perfect presentations that they believe are the true marks of a fraud. They are looking for someone who remembers what it was like to be where they are. They want to identify with a leader who not only has been there, but has found a way out. The postmodern minister need not try to sell him or herself as anything more than he or she is: a person, called by God, gifted by the Holy Spirit, and prone to wander. How do we get there? How we view ourselves will say a lot about how we want our congregation to view us. In a lot of ways, we control the picture that they have of us. Consider a couple of seemingly insignificant things:

1. Where do you sit on Sunday morning? If you are like most preachers, you occupy the "preacher's chair" on stage or the front pew where no one else dares to venture. Consider sitting "among the people." While this might seem petty, think about what it would communicate to someone who is new to your church when you are worshiping with him or her.

2. How high above the congregation is the platform from which

you speak? Is it significantly higher than where the people in the congregation sit? The visual message that you communicate is that you are "above" them. If it is structurally possible, consider a platform that is more at the level of the congregation.

3. How many barriers (i.e., communion table, pulpit, flowers, etc.) are between you and the seats in the worship center? If we want to be accessible, then we need to visually communicate that we are. Consider coming out from behind those barriers.

4. Where do you stand at the end of the Sunday morning service? Do you stand at the door and shake as many hands as you can, or do you blend in with the rest of the congregation becoming just one of many? Most people who come to your church want to shake your hand. It makes them feel good to know that you have seen them. If our goal is to move people into ministry, wouldn't it be better if people felt more obliged to talk to those around them after the service rather than talking to you. Granted, this will cut down on the accolades that you receive week in and week out, but it will also communicate to the people that there is more than one person in the room through which the church moves. People who have real issues will seek you out, and you will be able to devote intentional time to praying with and helping the hurting sheep.

To you, these may seem meaningless, but the amount of separation that you communicate to your congregation is indirectly (and directly) proportional to the amount of "esteem" to which they will hold you. We are not only trying to communicate the Word of God to postmoderns, we are also trying to break down the misconceptions that they have of professional ministers. Postmoderns reject the separation of clergy and congregation. They reject it because they know that it isn't true. They know that you are not holier than they are, and they want you to recognize it as well. More importantly, they need the person who helps direct their spiritual growth to communicate relevancy to them. They need to see the relevancy of the message first to you, and secondly to them. You are able to do that both verbally and nonverbally.

I heard someone say one time, "You can't be the life of the party on Saturday night and convict the congregation of their sin on Sunday morning." While that may be true to a certain degree, it would seem that the gap between the paid clergy and the congregation is closing. People no longer expect the minister to be the most holy man in the room. They need to know that this minister who is telling them what is right and wrong in God's eyes on Sunday, understands that it is sometimes difficult to apply that Monday. They need to see the vulnerability and humanity of their leader.

We have countless examples of the vulnerability of leadership. Paul expressed his vulnerability in almost every letter that he wrote. He anguished over the competing forces that were affecting how he lived. He wrote, "For in my inner being I delight in God's law; but I see another law at work in the members of my body, waging war against the law of my mind and making me a prisoner of the law of sin" (Rom. 7:22f). The struggle of the flesh and the Spirit is nothing new. Even Jesus let his followers in on his struggle between divinity and humanity. No one understood the hopelessness of humanity more than he did. Being fully God and yet fully human, he was able to grasp our condition to its fullest extent. In the Garden of Gethsemane, on the night he was betrayed, we get to see a brief glimpse of that struggle. He didn't keep it inside for only him to see, he revealed his anguish to his disciples when he told them, "My soul is overwhelmed with sorrow to the point of death" (Matt. 26:38). We all struggle with lust and greed and pride and envy. Just attend a preachers' conference and listen. The attendance of all of our churches jumps exponentially when we all get together. As our brother Paul exclaimed, "What a wretched man I am!" If we are going to reach this and the following generations, then we need to get a grip on the position of minister. This is not to say that ministers need to stand up every week and list all of the sins they have committed, but surely when we are teaching on lust, we can somehow let the congregation know that we are vulnerable, just as they are.

TEACHABLE MOMENTS

We are guides, directing people through the triumphs and trials of life; showing them life through a lens that many have not had the privilege of looking through. The job of the minister is moving from one who is a teacher of many, to one who finds teachable moments with a few. We cannot realize such a role if the sum total of our job is seen in how dynamic our sermons are, or how efficiently our church structure is run. We must get out from behind the mahogany tower and into the lives of the people who are lost in their search for significance.

> The job of the minister is moving towards finding teachable moments with a few.

What you will find is that postmoderns are desperate for this kind of personal interaction. While you cannot walk hand in hand with all of them, you can surely do it with a few. What you will also find in this new role is that you will not only be able to lead, but you will also be led. I meet with eight men, both single and married, twice a month for breakfast. It is one of the highlights of my week. We talk about life issues like career decisions and relationships. We talk about their lives and the decisions and issues that face them, and we journey together through one teachable moment after another.

What I find is that I am more aware of what it is like to

live life outside of the walls of the church. I am better able to grasp what it is like to live like most people live in a world that isn't kind to the philosophy of life that we share. To deal with bosses and debt and all of the things that people who are on the journey deal with. And I find, in my guidance, that I am able also to recognize growth areas in my own life as well. This helps me to be a more relevant leader. As I said earlier, one of the criticisms that postmoderns have of the church is that no one, especially the preacher, has a good grasp of the daily issues that they deal with. I wonder if maybe that is because we never take the time to ask. This philosophy of teachable moments has also made me a better preacher in that I am able to relate to the church community.

Finding moments to relate spiritual truths in everyday life is something that we as "professional ministers" have lost sight of. We dismiss our lack of real world contact with excuses of having responsibility to lead the sheep and that we are trying to help others to accomplish those tasks. But in many ways, we don't know what people in our congregations deal with on a weekly and daily basis. Our roles must change if we are ever to fully embrace the culture and people in the world in which we find ourselves ministering.

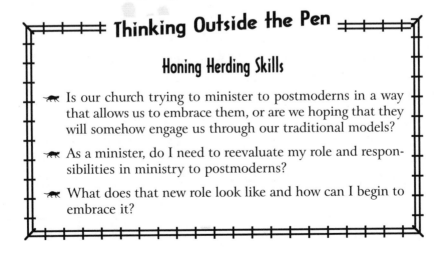

Thinking Outside the Pen

Honing Herding Skills

- Is our church trying to minister to postmoderns in a way that allows us to embrace them, or are we hoping that they will somehow engage us through our traditional models?

- As a minister, do I need to reevaluate my role and responsibilities in ministry to postmoderns?

- What does that new role look like and how can I begin to embrace it?

Learning How to Build In before Building Out

Cats and their human counterparts come with their individual personalities which have been molded by genetics and environment. If we want to develop a productive relationship with them, we need to understand where they're coming from and work with their personality in order to develop them into a functioning part of the vision we have for the future. This requires time, effort, patience, a willingness to work with them, and lots of love, but the rewards we reap not only in their lives, but ours and the church body's as well, will be well worth the huge investment we make in the beginning.

Each year I (Jeff) lead a group of people from our church to Mexico for missions work. For the past five years we have gone to the same city. Our first year, the missionary we work with took us to the downtown area of the city for some sightseeing. As we drove, he pointed out a particular building that was being constructed by the government for office space. The government was looking to lease the space for revenue. He commented that they were building it the way we do in the States and from what I could see, it certainly was going to be much different from the other buildings that dotted the landscape.

The next year, during the course of our trip, the missionary took the group on the same drive downtown. As we passed by the new building, it looked beautiful. It had a modern, American, architectural feel, was ten-stories high, and from what I could see, it looked finished. I asked him if the building was being used, and he said no. I asked him why, and he told me that when they were building it, many people from the town would go and watch the construction crew at work. Early on in the process, they had problems with a crack in the foundation. He went on to tell me that because of their desire to complete the building and start collecting revenue, they decided to take their chances and build on the cracked foundation. Because of that, the government spent millions of dollars and two years to construct a building that is still empty, years later. Their failure to take extra time on the foundation cost them a useless structure in the end.

LAYING A STRONG FOUNDATION

Developing and empowering leaders in the postmodern culture will hold many of the same challenges. In the previous chapter, we discussed how the role of the minister must change in order to meet the needs of the emerging culture. The next step in the journey is to build strong spiritual foundations in people so they can invest in the lives of others. With postmoderns, we are dealing with people who have cracked foundations or no foundations at all, who are able to understand little about their own faith, let alone lead others in the discovery of their faith. As leaders, we must concern ourselves with the process of laying a strong foundation in people so that we do not construct monuments that look good on the outside but are useless for the purpose for which they have been built.

The process of foundation-building is a long one. It takes time and effort with *individuals* not large groups. I believe that is why it is often neglect-ed if not over-looked all togeth-er. A young adults "service" seems to be a very popular form of ministry in churches all over the country. We regularly have visitors who stop by our worship time in order to observe what we do. They want to acquire our music and scout our program. Unfortunately, what they are observing is a building in process, with the foundation work already finished. They think if they can have good music, video clips, and candles, they will also have a successful young adults' ministry.

> We must not construct useless monuments that only look good on the outside.

Those visitors always direct questions to me that deal with our program. How long have you been doing it, how many people were around when you started, how long is the service, how long do you talk, and so on. They then believe they can take that information, go back to their church and reproduce what they have observed. Inevitably they become frustrated and often little results of well-intentioned effort. Common Ground as we have it today is a result of two years of foundation building.

Early in my ministry, I spent considerable time reading about empowerment and team lead-ership. I learned how successful ministry was more about a collective journey toward holiness and less about hierarchical, "I'm in charge, follow me" egotism. Because of that, I endeav-ored early in my very young career to share what God had placed on my heart with individuals—not only to minister to them, but to allow them to come alongside of me and share in the vision of ministry that I had in mind. I spent a lot of time with people and shared with them my passion to give young adults the opportunity to connect with Jesus as their Lord and with a community of disciples with whom they could live.

Some people didn't share that same vision. Some weren't interested in what I was interested in or didn't agree with the specific method of ministry to young adults that I did. Eventually, I found four people who did share the same passion and vision, and together we began our journey. Along the way, I shared with them new ideas and possible program changes, but rarely if ever did I tell them what we were going to do next. We shared in that process as a team.

The traditional, "professional minister" model that most churches hold is a cumbersome structure from which to work. When the team is made up of ten volunteers and one "paid professional," the tendency is for the staff minister to assume control and direct the building process. He becomes the foreman for the project, and because he is a professional and holds a seminary degree, we assume he also must be the one through whom God will speak and work. The professional, the foreman, simply lines up skilled (deacons) and unskilled (anyone else who will volunteer) workers to build the building that he has envisioned. This is the modern paradigm of leadership. Leonard Sweet comments, "Leadership in the modern world was the power of charisma and command. Only a few people had it. These were gifts. Leadership in the postmodern world is collaboration and interaction. Everybody has it. These are learnings."[1]

> In the new paradigm, leadership looks more like a design team.

In the postmodern paradigm, leadership looks more like a design team working together to form and construct the building together. Each member contributes not only to the construction, but also to the design. The team makes decisions on shape and color, material and building methods. They share in all of the decisions that go into leading a church and building a building. The team and the process of collaboration become as important as the resulting product of ministry. Many church leaders miss a wonderful ministry opportunity in not taking the time to invest in the collaborative, team-focused process of leadership. We miss the opportunity to learn, the privilege to disagree and to re-solve issues together. We miss the relationships that are built as we overcome trials and celebrate triumphs. We miss the joy of the collective journey that is the body of Christ. The church, under the headship of Christ Jesus, forms the body. For us to separate ourselves from that body in order to build the church misses the point of the body altogether. First Corinthians 12:12 states, "The body is a unit, though it is made up of many parts; and though all its parts are many, they form one body. So it is with Christ." To assume that the minister is the head of the church is to deny the God-ordained makeup of the body. There is a new paradigm of leadership on the horizon and it involves the community and celebrates the process and the journey over the product. In this new paradigm of leadership, the postmodern leader will serve as the facilitator that helps all parts of the body realize and express their part in the body. We will be people of empowerment and collaboration.

The team and the process of collaboration become as important as the result.

If efficiency is the goal, this new paradigm in leadership is not for you. It is not the most efficient way to lead a team when the end goal in mind is a well-run, finely tuned, administratively flawless organization that can be diagrammed and dissected. But when the product we are looking for is a fully devoted disciple of Christ Jesus, then the process of disciple building becomes all the more important. In this new culture of leadership, we must be concerned about building *in* before we build *out*. Postmoderns will lead and follow best when there is an opportunity to share in the process. I found very early that this was true.

A DESIRE FOR DISCIPLINE

Not only is the new framework for leadership changing, the people that we are developing are different as well. The process of training people for ministry may be attainable, but what happens when we begin to recruit postmoderns to be involved with us in the process? What you will find will certainly frustrate you as well.

I host a membership class every month for new people to learn the basics of what our church believes, ask questions, and meet other people who are new to our church. One night, as we were introducing ourselves and how we came to the church, a young woman told her story. She had just moved to town, and was looking for a new church home. Her first visit to any church in the city, and there are many, was to ours. She said, "I have found my home." I was amazed that one visit to one church in one week could flesh out that decision so definitively. I was feeling rather proud of my church at that point and chalked her comment up to an obvious gift of discernment. We continued the class and at the conclusion she told me she was ready to join. Wow, I must have really done a good job! She signed our membership covenant and was on her way, and I was on cloud nine with another notch in my church membership belt. I never saw her or talked with her again. I called and e-mailed and wrote letters, but to no avail. She had vanished as quickly as she had appeared.

> We must shift our focus from building out to building in.

I learned a valuable lesson from that experience about the commitment level, or lack thereof, of postmoderns. The flaw in my approach was that I helped her continue that attitude by focusing more on the breadth of the church rather than the depth of the people in the church. If we are going to build healthy, spiritually mature Christian leaders, then we must shift our focus from building out to building in. We must challenge the mind-set of noncommitment and challenge postmoderns to begin to live lives of discipline. Richard Foster in his book *Celebration of Discipline* said it like this: "Superficiality is the curse of our age. The doctrine of instant satisfaction is a primary spiritual problem. The desperate need today is not for a greater number of intelligent people, or gifted people, but for deep people."[2]

Postmoderns come by this attitude honestly. We have never been required to commit too much of anything in our lifetime. I am not a sociologist, but I attribute some of this attitude to our lack of participation in a major, national campaign. The generations before us had commitment and discipline built into their lives because they found themselves in the middle of war. Conflict forces us to choose a side, to take a stand either for or against. Generations before us found they had to band together in order to defend their freedom from outside, hostile forces. Postmoderns have never been required to put their lives on the line for anything. Because of that we find them committing to nothing, except themselves.

You can hold differing opinions and views, you can do whatever you want whenever you want, and others will care less, until it infringes on your ability to get what you want. Just look at the strategy of presidential candidates over the last three elections: appearances on *Saturday Night Live, The Tonight Show, MTV*, the Internet, and every other medium that the postmodern culture uses. The candidates recognize the political apathy of the twenty-something voter and are trying to win them with a perception of relevance. So if postmoderns don't care about anything except themselves, as a church we are fooling ourselves if we think they are going to participate in our top-heavy, management-focused ministry system. What value does a meeting or a "program" have for them? They give us their answer to that question in the form of their absence.

Like the Mexican builders, what we need to do is to take some time and do a little foundation building. Trying to add postmodern thinkers to the modern structure of the church will simply render your building useless and you frustrated. We have to start somewhere though, and I believe our starting point begins with the ancient art of discipleship. "Ancient art?" you ask. "Our church has a discipleship program right now," you say. Many churches do employ the term "discipleship" in their programming, but I wonder how we are doing at the ancient art of disciple making.

It began with Jesus, who found twelve men who were willing to sacrifice all that they had for the cause. They ate together, traveled together, prayed together, served together, learned together, suffered together, did virtually everything that people do together for three years, after which, their Discipler left them and gave them specific instructions: "Go and make disciples." Not plant churches, not build buildings, not plan programs, but make disciples. I believe the foundation for reaching the future generations will be seen in our willingness to disciple individuals through the process of becoming fully devoted followers of Jesus.

You agree, you are nodding your head, you are ready to move on, but wait. Don't dismiss this concept so soon. How is the organizational structure of your church geared? Is it geared to reach many or to teach one? You see, filling your pews is not disciple making. Breaking attendance records, having the best Easter pageant, filling the church with activity and people all may look great but fall short of both making disciples for Jesus and connecting with postmoderns. Because, you see, as we program,

Filling your pews is not disciple making.

as we gather people, we force them into a dependency on us as the *institution* of the church. We never allow them to mature to the extent that they are themselves making disciples. They may be inviting their neighbors to the Easter show, or to the Sunday morning show, but they are not making disciples. Postmoderns don't need what we are peddling, and so they will find what they need from someone or somewhere else.

The depth and strength of the foundation of our churches in the future will be dependent on our commitment to the art of disciple-making today. The primary reason for our need to build disciples among postmoderns is that we are dealing with people who have been raised without an assumed moral standard for right and wrong. All that they believe in and all that their philosophy of life is grounded in is post-Christian. They have no real understanding of absolute morality and because of that, they cannot speak our language. They need to be trained and taught about what following Jesus Christ is all about. So the church's response is that we have Sunday school and Bible study, and if they want to know about it, they can come and drink our coffee and eat our doughnuts and listen to our teachers. And what we miss, what we fail to see, is that our methods are all wrong.

Disciple making begins with a relationship. It begins with someone who loves Jesus and loves other people. It begins with a burden in the heart of a believer to share his or her life and experience with someone else. It involves a fifty-year-old woman, whose children are out of the house and independent to reach back to a twenty-two-year-old single mom who needs someone to talk to, to lean on, and to cry with. Disciple making is first about developing a relationship. This is the hardest part of the process. When we talk about discipling postmoderns, we are talking about a messy and sometimes uncomfortable situation. Disciple making involves taking time to be around people who are not like you, who hold opinions that are different from yours, who live their lives differently than you do. It involves stepping outside of your zone of comfort and into a zone of confusion and chaos, but in the end the result will be more rewarding than you could ever imagine. Disciple making means to be there when this person whom you have been praying for and sharing with gets it for the first time—when she sees the beauty of a relationship with Jesus and how contentment in life can be found in a relationship with him. It is worth every minute that you will invest. And in the end, you will begin to build depth, deep people who now share your vision and passion and are ready to reproduce themselves.

Disciple making costs you something. I could guess that Jesus would much rather have stayed in heaven. He would much rather have continued his life of divinity among the divine. Instead, he chose to live out his divinity among the disobedient. And we will never understand what that must have been like. Fighting, arguing, and betraying, this band of would-be disciples certainly looked better in the end than they did in the beginning. Jesus was patient with them; he brought them along slowly, not giving them more than they could handle and yet challenging them when they needed it. He taught them relationally. He instructed them about this new way of life as they were living the old one. The problem that we have with this "art" is that it takes time. It may not look good at the end of the year when you evaluate the numbers. It may involve your getting out of the office and into the coffee shop. It won't look like an impressive building at first, but in the end it will be occupied. Disciple making will be the foundation of the church in the postmodern world in which we are finding ourselves.

Disciple making will be the foundation of the church in the postmodern world.

The new structure for this art will also be important. In the past, the church has found the structure of the classroom to be most effective in communicating the lessons of Christianity. We passed out outlines and diagrams and disseminated information so that we could equip rational thinkers with life skills from the Bible. In the future, the community will be the structure, with relationships being the preferred mode of communication. The small-group community becomes the structure through which we journey together. Notice the shift—the shift from the church expressing herself as a gathered mass to expressing herself as a scattered few. The growth of our church and the development of our leaders will be best accomplished as we bind people together in disciple-making relationships and give them room to grow in the small group. It is my belief that small group life will be critical for all churches in this new millennium, not just as an optional program that has an equal standing with the men's banquet and VBS, but the hub through which we grow disciples and flow ministry.

Here is a simple way to compare the old paradigm with the new. In the old paradigm, the corporate celebration is the most important aspect of the church. From that gathering, ministry involvement flows (i.e., small groups, Sunday school, ministry teams, etc.). This simple diagram illustrates it:

In the new paradigm, the small group becomes the vehicle through which all ministry flows. It becomes the primary focal point of involvement with all other ministry flowing out of individual small groups. Corporate worship is still a priority in this model. It simply is not the most important aspect of the church but an equal pillar on the same level as service, mission, Bible teaching, and other ministries.

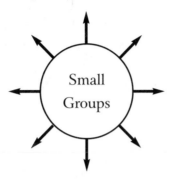

From this structure your entire ministry flows, built on the foundation of relational discipleship and training. When you have a need that arises in your congregation, you go to your small groups to meet that need. When someone enters your church and wants to know how to get involved, the first step is a small group. When you encourage people to share in the privilege of evangelism, you encourage them to expose those they hope to reach to people in the small group. Because intimacy and relationships can be built and nurtured best in the smaller context and because postmoderns are searching for just such connections, the small group will be essential for the next church.

I already can hear the skeptics: "That's fine for young single people, but what about when they get married and grow up? They won't need that same relational component then, will they?" You are thinking, "You just wait until they grow up; they will be just like us." I know from where you are drawing that conclusion, but the difference in the postmoderns and their modern parents is this. Previous generations saw relationships as a need. When they were younger and living on their own, they needed people to help curb their loneliness. What usually happened was, once a person got married, the need for companionship was met through the spouse, and so the small group that previously scratched that relational itch was no longer needed.

We are dealing with something in the postmodern culture that goes beyond a need. Postmoderns have similar needs for companionship, but they find value in themselves by finding value in their community. The scary part is that the community will take on many shapes and sizes. The club scene has characterized the community of the nineties to the present. People have been flocking to clubs, shedding individuality, and taking on the persona of the community where they find themselves. They aren't just purple hair, drug addicted, homeless teens either. In fact, I had the opportunity to attend a rave with an urban ministry team in our city. I was shocked when we walked in and saw parents from upper-middle-class suburban communities in minivans dropping their kids off. The club culture is not so much about the music or dancing, but about the value system from which postmoderns operate.

They express themselves in community. Their parents expressed themselves in their accomplishments, in their abilities and gifts. The goal of the eighties was building big business and making lots of money. People found their self worth in the monuments to capitalism they constructed and the dominion that those monuments afforded them. Many of the new church plants are meeting in the buildings that illustrate this as a practical example. They are finding warehouses that are abandoned, shopping malls that have gone under, superstores that no longer sell products, and are using them as a place to meet. Interestingly, these empty buildings are the products of the construction of the previous generations. Corporate downsizing, cut backs, and shut downs have caused these once lucrative places of business now to sit empty. The values have changed.

Postmoderns find satisfaction in themselves by finding a place to belong, a group of people to identify with. Ever wonder why parents are so concerned with their children when they graduate from college, move in with a bunch of guys, and appear to be going nowhere? It is because moderns are evaluating the lives of their children with the wrong lens. They are hoping that Junior will grow up someday to be just like them, not recognizing that Junior will never be like them—not because he doesn't love and respect his parents, not because he isn't grateful for the example that his mom and dad have given him, but because his values are different from their values. Because of that, his life pursuits will be different than theirs were.

A good illustration of this would be seen in the X Games. The X Games is an annual gathering of young postmoderns and beyond doing what they do best, dangerous and nontraditional sports. The beauty of the X Games is that it is *not* so much about who wins or who loses. When you watch the games, you could even get the impression that there isn't supposed to be a winner or loser. There isn't any fighting, no trash talking, and it resembles a preseason exhibition, rather than the real thing. You can see it in all of the athletes' faces. The joy for the athletes is the competition itself and the community that is built as people with similar skills and interests bind themselves together in the journey of the sport.

The beauty of the sport is seen in the *story* of the community and the individuals that make it up. The human-interest stories take up as much time as the sport itself. Unlike the modern sports of basketball, football, soccer, and the like, the X Games celebrates the journey to the pinnacle of the sport with each individual sharing in the process of helping community excel. Playbooks aren't hidden; they are shared. Strategy isn't secret; it is talked about openly with other competitors. Competitors don't view others as the enemy, but as their *family*. You don't see fights in the X Games because everyone is pulling for everyone else. If I can't win, I hope my buddy does. This is the value system of future generations. It is more than a need to be filled and noticed, but a desire to be quenched.

The Church Responds

The church responds by recognizing the needs of post-moderns and then facilitating an environment where those needs can be met. Your ability to embrace the needs of this culture and meet those needs with new and relevant relationships will determine the effectiveness of your congrega-tion in the future. That is why the idea of starting a "service" for postmoderns instead of first building a foun-dation rarely is effective. This ap-proach is simply taking the value of the modern world and trying to make it "look" and "feel" postmodern. In fact, it will take a lot of your time and effort and will frustrate you in the end. We as a church need to embrace these next generations through the values that they have with no intention of dressing them up to look like us, and then communicate the gospel to them the way that they will best receive it. That method is the *relationship*.

Your ability to address the relationship issue will determine your effectiveness.

---

[1] Leonard Sweet, *Aqua Church: Essential Leadership Arts for Piloting Your Church in Today's Fluid Culture* (Loveland CO: Group Publishing, 1999), p. 192.

[2] Richard Foster, *Celebration of Discipline: The Path to Spiritual Growth* (San Francisco: HarperCollins, 1998), p. 1.

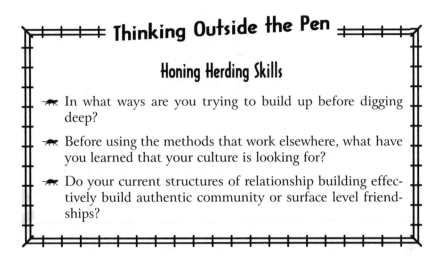

Thinking Outside the Pen

Honing Herding Skills

🐾 In what ways are you trying to build up before digging deep?

🐾 Before using the methods that work elsewhere, what have you learned that your culture is looking for?

🐾 Do your current structures of relationship building effectively build authentic community or surface level friendships?

Recruitment of Leaders Takes More Than a Sign-up Sheet

Herding cats will require a gentle and personal touch. Cats do not respond well to overbearing, domineering, and heavy-handed threats. They either want to do something or not, period. A cat hater will say that no amount of begging with the promise of reward will convince them to do what you want. In the postmodern church we must enlist Christians to use their God-given talents as servants in ministry. The military will likely never "recruit" cats as they have dogs. The church will need to recruit everyone!

This is Jeff asking, Why is it so hard to recruit leaders? If you are like the average church in America and you have twenty percent of your people in ministry, then you have probably settled for "this is as good as it's going to get." We can get them in the door, we know how they respond to programming, but why can't we get them to help us? Wouldn't it be great if people were coming to you, excited about their relationship with Jesus and eager to help serve others in ministry? We can achieve such a model, not just with twenty percent, but with a large majority in each of our congregations. But again, as with everything in life, we may have to change the way we classify "service" in the Body of Christ.

For so long, participation in the church has meant that you have a ministry responsibility. More specifically, you have a ministry responsibility within the local congregation that somehow keeps the church running. Our job is to make sure all the positions are filled. What happens as our church grows and as people discover their giftedness, we find that we don't have enough jobs for everyone. So we create new ones. New structures and leaders and tasks to be accomplished in order to support the mission and ministry of the church. Then the person for whom we created the position decides to move on or move out and we panic. A hole has sprung in our system and someone needs to place the proverbial finger in the dike! We beg, we plead, we offer cash, and finally we get someone to fill the spot. We acclimate him to the hierarchy of leadership and "release" him for ministry requiring only a detailed report and board meeting every month whether he needs to report or not. Soon he is burnt to a crisp or he drowns in ministry. No one knows for sure what the ministry is supposed to accomplish and certainly no one wants to be a part of it. And so you preach again and again on the importance of ministry involvement and you advertise the holes that you desperately need filled. Have we ever stopped to think that maybe only twenty percent of the people are involved in our ministry structure because that is really the only meaningful, necessary ministry that takes place inside the church walls? Have we ever thought that high turnover might be due to a lack of interest in maintaining a program or ministry with no real mission?

> High turnover might be due to a lack of real ministry purpose in what we do.

There is something about authentic worship, genuine community, and a God-inspired mission that causes postmoderns to get excited. We have talked about the first two. This third piece is a natural progression of the discipleship process. I believe it is that way for all people, but in the context of postmodern ministry it will simply look different. I believe that when we teach people to follow Jesus because of his grace for them, then they will be motivated to seek God's face in worship. I believe that as they grow in this new life, their old life relationships will leave them empty and they will seek out new expressions to help fill the void. Finally, I believe that when we truly understand and take hold of the mission of Jesus, we will see that it involves us. Each and every Christian follower expressing herself through her unique, Holy Spirit giftedness in the body of Christ. This is the discipleship model that Jesus taught us, and that we have been charged to reproduce.

The issue then becomes one of application. The modern church follows this progression primarily within the walls of the church building. We worship on Sunday mornings at either first or second service. During the other hour, we go to Sunday school and we build what we believe to be community. Then on alternating Sundays, we skip one of those options and work in the nursery, serve communion, or participate in one of many different tasks that have been created to get our people "involved." Don't misunderstand me, because we need certain people to count the offering and serve the communion and help in the necessary maintenance of the church. Some of these tasks involve spiritual gifts; many just involve a servant's heart and attitude of responsibility to the community in which we are involved. But what about a different understanding of the mission? How can we take the principle of relationships in the context of small groups and teach people about the mission that God has for them as his children?

The early church was a scattered church. They were scattered largely because of persecution. Though this may have seemed undesirable to the early church, it appears as though they were more effective in carrying out their mission than we are today. I think we dismiss the model of the church scattered in small groups and meeting in homes. The central focus of the church didn't revolve around the place where the newsletter originates. The people understanding that the mission of the church was on their shoulders made it effective. If they were going to proclaim the gospel, they were all to share in the responsibility. It wasn't until the third century that churches even had buildings. What happened next was tragic! The organization of the church took over and the mission of the church was never the same. Christians no longer felt personal responsibility in the mission. The church was reduced to the level of a government agency with red tape and committees as the ruling order.

The church struggles today in many ways because we have taken our eyes off of the mission. We have lost sight of what the church is supposed to be about. We have settled for a model that is well maintained and requires a lot of people, but really doesn't accomplish the task at hand. We have allowed people to be a part of the church without functioning as a member of Christ's Body. We have dropped the standards.

The good news is that the postmodern generation wants to be involved. They don't merely want to *attend* your church, they want to *be* the church. They want to read the Word and flesh it out in their everyday, walking-around lives. They can't do it though unless they are given the framework through which to do it, and the traditional church doesn't offer that framework. Participation in the mod-

> We have allowed people to be a part of the church without functioning as a member of Christ's body.

ern church never gets many people involved in life-transforming ministry.

Postmoderns are basically illiterate when it comes to the Bible, and they will gladly admit this fact. We see this as a negative, and in many ways it is, but consider this: As you begin to disciple just one person, and as he embraces salvation through a relationship with Jesus Christ, he wants to serve. That is the natural outcome of the regenerating work of the Holy Spirit. He doesn't know that committee meetings are supposed to be a part of the tradition of the church, so he serves. No one ever told him that he couldn't involve himself in meaningful, life-changing ministry until he was married with children and had a mortgage, so he serves. He actually believes that when he received the gift of the Holy Spirit, he was then a part of the "royal priesthood," so he exercises his priestly rights and he serves. He doesn't do it in the traditional church because the church requires such things; he cannot wait to tell others about his love for his Lord and to serve others the way that Christ served him.

In Europe there is a movement underway in the young adult community. It is being characterized as a spiritual awakening. Young, inexperienced Christian men and women are planting churches all over Europe. Thousands are coming to know Jesus through this movement, and it is all outside of the structure of the traditional church.

Postmoderns have an activist mentality. They want to participate in helping to meet other people's needs with their own hands. They don't find ministry fulfillment in simply knowing that a percentage of their tithe goes to missions. In fact they would rather take that percentage to the missionaries with their own hands. They want to simplify their lives and work less, volunteer more. A surprising number of women in our church want to stay at home and raise their children, bucking the tradition of their modern mothers who worked more than any generation before them. So how are we helping them? How are we taking the desire for community and authentic worship of God and giving them a way to express those passions to serve?

Consider this. You have a need in your children's ministry (who doesn't?). You are constantly losing willing workers to burnout and to their feeling that this isn't their "gift" (translation: "I don't like this anymore, and this is the most spiritual way for me to save face"). What if you could go to your small groups and ask each of them to take a week, in rotation, to provide you with the hands that are needed to accomplish this vital ministry in your church? These people become the primary labor force of your church. You still have room for those people who do feel gifted and led to teach and train children. If your church has a small-group strategy, then eventually, a majority of your congregation will be involved, creating many groups. Our small groups will work two to three times a year in the children's ministry and we will cover all 52 weeks. We will have people who are gifted, truly gifted, teaching our children while our small groups provide crowd control and love.

This is one example of the many uses that small groups have and that you can accomplish if you are a church of small groups. The neat part about this is that a new believer sees the importance of "ownership" in his church alongside a mature Christian who has already come to that point. Your elders, your staff, all part of small groups, will take their turns participating as their group does its part.

In many ways it goes back to the decentralization of the church and our ability to equip people for service. We must empower them to carry out the mission of the church without binding them to church structure. For years we have been painting the picture of ministry for people. We have been reproducing those prints ad nauseam all over the country and the world. Church after church is jumping on board the next train trying to copy the form and function of the new "megachurch." The problem isn't Jesus, it's that our taste is out of style. Let's try this. Instead of giving people paint-by-number books with four colors and a brush, let's try to give them a blank canvas and an infinitely wide pallet of colors and help them learn to paint. We need to allow the Holy Spirit within the body of Christ room to operate. We need to teach people, train people, and then trust people to go out into the world and share the message of Jesus through word and through deed.

This may mean that people will be a part of your fellowship and participating in ministry outside of *your* ministry structure. Praise God for that! When this begins to happen *en masse*, then you know you are doing something right. You are an equipper. The most fulfilling and the most awakening moment in the journey of our church was the moment that I heard about a ministry that was taking root and touching peoples lives and I had nothing to do with it. I was excited by the fact that they didn't run anything by *me* or ask for *my* advice, but they just did it. I was also saddened by the fact that they *didn't* run anything by me or ask for my advice; they just did it! The best thing that could possibly happen to the church is for people to start functioning as whole, healthy members. This will change our management-heavy structures. This will eliminate the need for one minister for every 75-100 people. This will give you less direct oversight into the details of the church and open up more opportunity for prayer, the study of the Word, and one-on-one discipleship.

This type of structure is a paradigm shift for many churches. It will take a lot of time and prayer for your congregation and your leadership to embrace such a change.

Moving from a church *with* small groups into a church *of* small groups is never easy! What would be the reaction if you were to tell your elders that in a year, the only activity you wanted them doing would be prayer and shepherding? If you set an expectation that from now on no "business" would be taken care of in the elders' meeting, and the only discussion would be centered on the spiritual health of your congregations, what would happen? I know what you mean. And though you may want to get there, you are a long way away. I believe it begins with the small-group structure and trickles up to free your elders to do what they have been called to do, which is to shepherd.

The church is changing right before our eyes regardless of whether you have yours open or shut. I believe the churches who will continue to minister the Word of God effectively in the coming years will be churches who understand that a big church is not necessarily a healthy church. I believe that the megachurch will be exchanged for the metachurch. A church made up of an infinite number of smaller churches. In this model, churches will be able to develop foundations that are deep and solid. Churches who concern themselves with this idea of discipleship and ministry through home fellowships will be better aware of the needs of their congregation. They will be much more easily mobilized in times of crisis. They will find that people will begin to rise to the expectation level that we set for them.

I know of a church that is beginning this process of meta-sizing their church. While they are excited about the possibilities, they are certainly aware of the enormous task at hand. They are an old and storied congregation who have certainly been open to change over the years, but now face more than a programmatic change. The philosophy of "church" is changing for them: how they define it, how they see their role, and how they understand their call as disciples. I don't think they understand the extent to which they will be challenged and moved. I know I don't. They see this process, not as another program to be added, but as a change in the culture of their church.

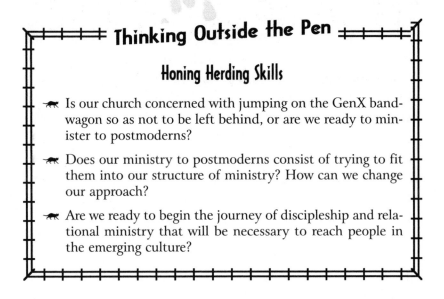

Thinking Outside the Pen

Honing Herding Skills

- Is our church concerned with jumping on the GenX bandwagon so as not to be left behind, or are we ready to minister to postmoderns?

- Does our ministry to postmoderns consist of trying to fit them into our structure of ministry? How can we change our approach?

- Are we ready to begin the journey of discipleship and relational ministry that will be necessary to reach people in the emerging culture?

"If Someone Will Just Work in the Nursery, I'll Put the Gun Down!"

Motivating a cat? No way. As we discussed in previous chapters, you are barking up the wrong animal. You can scream, you can cry, you can hold your breath. You can plead, you can be nice, you can speak baby talk but you cannot motivate an independent cat! Then we apply the same tactics to church leadership. They won't work. Selling our leadership vision from now on is like trying to herd cats. There is hope if we can learn the art of appropriate presentation.

Understanding that we need to empower leaders is not the difficult part. Asking people to serve is not even that challenging, but motivating leaders to complete the work with the same enthusiasm that you would have is the greatest hurdle. Dealing with potential leaders influenced by a postmodern age only intensifies the tension. Often they hold to their own agenda, timetable, and version of what is important. Simply telling them "because I said so" won't serve as proper motivation.

Future leaders of the church need *motivation and direction* in the ministries to which they are called. Our previous assumptions will only impede the process. For instance, many of us take a look at the upcoming generations and assume by their whimsical approach to life and work that they are *lazy*. Conversely, postmoderns would say that rather than imitate the previous generations that lived driven and compulsive lifestyles, they are carefree and have *shunned materialism*.

Equally the previous methods of motivation will serve us no longer. Manipulation with guilt or rewards will not give us the results we seek. In the world of volunteers and post-modernity the use of carrots and whips that have satisfied corporate management will only leave the church void of authentic servants. Today's leaders will not work out of their passion to simply "get the job done" for accomplishment's sake. They want greater significance. In an effort to work for more than just the betterment of a corporation, many young leaders are leaving well-paying jobs with stable companies to pursue positions with nonprofit organizations that seek to better humanity. One of our leaders came to me [Rusty] one day and said, "I just don't want to go home another Friday and realize I've given another week of my life to promoting a computer printer." He soon left that job and took a lesser-paying position with the Salvation Army.

PREVIOUS METHODS OF MOTIVATION

Pleading to the Masses

We have all tried to recruit, train, and motivate future leaders from the pulpit. Standing up, stating the problem, begging for assistance has left most of us empty handed. One method that has been used is to ask for volunteers to sign up at the information table. Another is to have them jot their names and numbers down on cards and drop them in the offering plate. And still another is just to beg for help and have them see you after the service while you are toweling off the tears. The only way many of us have found any success in this process is to ask so much that people volunteer out of pity or in an effort to get you to stop humiliating yourself. Sooner or later our constant begging will bring one benevolent soul out of the crowd to answer our cry for a nursery worker. It won't take long for that person to make it very obvious that she has no talent with children and she is finding her service experience miserable.

> Sooner or later our constant begging will bring one benevolent soul out of the crowd

Our college outreach program, "College Café," made a pledge to each student that every Sunday morning we would not only provide him or her with great music and a biblical message, but also a meal. We charged nothing for the food, but we did encourage donations of money or service in preparation. Usually once a month I would have to stand up and beg people for a dollar of their weekend money, an hour of their time for food set up, or a little bit of effort in the clean up. Each time I was met with no response. But the ironic thing was that when I went to students individually, told them what we were trying to do, explained to them our need, and asked for their help, they became interested in being involved. The problem often isn't that they lack drive, it's that they lack direction.

Teaching the Masses

Another method we often rely on is that of one-time instruction. We hold a meeting, we explain the job, and then we expect it to be done. But with postmoderns it isn't that cut and dried. Many of them have lacked the core teachings of responsibility and maturity because they grew up in dysfunctional homes. Plus, with the influence of a world that has rejected absolute truth, many have disengaged their minds and begun to rely solely upon their feelings. People with these handicaps require a mentoring style of motivation.

Several years ago a young man named Rich began to get involved with our ministry. He had grown up under difficult conditions, he was skeptical about church at best, and he feared accomplishing any task for fear it wouldn't be good enough. It wasn't enough for us as leaders to simply tell him the job and let him go. He needed to walk with others and learn the spirit of the job more than just the details. He began to spend great amounts of time with us, helping, learning, and often disappointing. Late for everything, no attention to detail, brash in his relationships, this was a difficult process to stay in, but nevertheless, we did. Many of our young adult leaders continued to mentor and train Rich realizing that often our words fell on deaf ears. We had to learn that leadership training in a postmodern world requires more than a pamphlet and a pep talk.

> We had to learn that leadership training requires more than a pamphlet and a pep talk.

New Methods for Motivation

Call Them to a Vision, not a Job

Have you ever compared the directions of a board game with the directions of a computer video game? Most board games were made during the modern era and their directions read that way. There is one objective, one way of getting there, and solid rules about the process. Many computer video games that postmoderns have grown up with provide them with multiple experiences. The directions read like a story that describes the history of the scenario, the danger that lies ahead, and the variety of encounters the person may have along the way. These directions cast a full picture rather than just a blueprint.[1] We tend to motivate postmodern leaders with modern methods. We detail the steps along the way but never paint a picture of "the where" we are heading, where we've been, and what excitement we may discover along the way. Rich Hurst described it this way: "The role of a leader is not to motivate someone else but to create environments where people can discover what God has called them to do."[2]

When calling a leader to a task, do not only tell the person what the job is and how it gets done, cast some vision for the job. Start by telling the potential leader what the need is and allowing him to create the vision: "There are literally thousands of young adults like you who don't come to church because they don't feel like church connects with them. Would you agree? We are trying to create such an environment where your friends who have never darkened the doors of a church can connect. What does that look like to you? What if we put together some type of service that communicated the truth of the gospel in such a way that you would be excited to bring your friends, and they would be excited to come back? Would you be willing to be part of a programming team that works together to create an experience that would connect the unconnected young adult to Christ and the church?" Suddenly this potential leader now knows the need and the goal by seeing a picture of what could be. Not only that, he gets to be involved in painting that picture.

Recently our human resource department conducted several interviews for different positions. Despite the differences in background, experience, and personality, one noticeable distinction between the candidates was one young woman's intent in interviewing us. She asked many questions about our philosophy of ministry, our core values, and our mission statement for the future. Our Director of Human Resources commented that this was beginning to become a consistent practice for young adults—they are just as curious about the vision of their future employment as the employer is in their ability.

Give your leaders a clear-cut picture of how their involvement will not only satisfy their desire to be a part of something important but will also allow them to catch a glimpse of how they can impact eternity. Finding some type of significance that is greater than a bottom line or material possessions is the underlying motivation for many of the young adults today. These leaders of tomorrow are more likely to be involved in the Peace Corps, Habitat for Humanity, and even short-term mission trips than generations before. This type of refocusing of priorities provides potential leaders who are thirsty for a vision of significance, not a job out of duty.

Create Teams, Not "To-Do" Lists

Tiger Woods is one of the greatest golfers of all time. We marvel at the tournaments he wins and the records he breaks, yet in spite of being at the height of his popularity, there is a retired basketball player that still has more market value. Even after he has left the limelight, people are still enamored with Michael Jordan. This six-time world champion from the Chicago Bulls may have a resume filled with records, yet by the time Tiger is finished he may hold even more. What is it that continues to draw us to Michael Jordan? We continue to be consumed with this amazing basketball player because we naturally gravitate toward teamwork. Sports fans watched as he matured from a one-man show into an innovative team player that elevated the level of play for everyone around him. This resonates with us because we work in jobs that require some degree of teamwork, and we live with a soul that craves authentic community. Hurst claims that there are two ways to begin new areas of ministry, specifically young adult ministry.

One is to say, "Let's start a group for people in their twenties," and then sit back and hope people

will come. The other is to involve young adults in
every process, from conception through execution.
Surprisingly, many churches never stop to ask people in their twenties what they'd like in a program.
This could be why so many programs fail.[3]

People want to be involved in the process and they want to do
this in a community-based team.

Jesus pointed out the two greatest needs that we have
when he gave us the two greatest commandments.[4] More than
anything else we need to have community with God and with
people. Whether or not we have people skills, are an extrovert,
or an introvert, we are truly satisfied when we are in a relationship with God and are "doing life" with each other. In
view of this, it is imperative that we call people to serve on a
team rather than execute a "to do" list.

Many churches have an eldership, church
board, or a select group of volunteers, that
handle the majority of the work. Most of these groups have
tasks for which they are responsible, i.e., communion, offering, and hospital visitation. They have annual committees
that meet to make policy, often divide and do ministry work
alone, and wonder why they watch the calendar for their tour
of duty to end. How different would things be if they were to
actually function as teams? Welcome teams, offering counting
teams, and auditorium clean up teams could meet thirty minutes prior to serving together, catch up on life issues, pray
together, and then serve as a team. It's easy to skip a chance
to work when that is all it is. It becomes more difficult to skip
this experience when you would miss being with the people
you do life with.

Recently one of our set-up teams for our postmodern
service changed the pace by moving to this level. What can be
a thankless job of heavy lifting and unnoticed clean up, set-up
work is often a difficult job to sell. But this team has been able

not only to attract members but to keep them due to their commitment to being involved in each other's lives. Whether it is prayer time after their work is done, or occasional parties to celebrate their team, people connect with this type of leadership. Just giving them a checklist of what needs to be done to keep us looking good isn't very attractive to anyone, let alone a postmodern young adult. They have better options for entertainment, but they have few options for community. That is what draws them and keeps them.

About forty years ago the leadership craze began. The last of modernity gave us the insight of several authors who reported what they had discovered as the hope of the business world. Ironically the majority of the material dealt with the individualization of training and the internalizing of evaluation. If we could detect personal internal weaknesses, spend time and training in correcting them, then we'd have better results with better individuals. Leadership found its problems and solutions inside of each individual.

Over the past ten years the first leadership authors of postmodernity are taking us in a different direction. The majority of their work is focusing on teamwork. Teams provide more energy, more intensity, and more accountability. We all find it easier to maintain a set of core values with a team than we do individually. Over the course of the next few years we will see the discussion of teamwork move from teams in the office to teams internationally. The Internet is causing the globalization of the marketplace and teams are consisting of members from all over the world. We cannot expect the young leaders that we hope to attract to be content to "just do a job"; they want community.

Use People's Skill, Not Just Their Sweat

Many times in recruitment and motivation I find myself looking for anyone with a pulse. It doesn't matter his or her age, ability, experience, or passion, I just need someone to fill this spot. And as a result we often have people who are passionate about working behind the scenes mis- matched with a job that requires them to lead a Bible Study. Or we will take an enthusiastic gifted communica- tor and place him in a room by himself filing curriculum. The question is not whether or not a person is humble enough to do whatever it takes for the good of the cause, the question is whether or not he should have to. After all, stifling someone's giftedness because we want him or her to do whatever it takes does nothing for the good of the cause, it only weakens a church.

> Many times I find myself looking for anyone with a pulse.

We further this type of motivation in several ways. First, use a spiritual gift assessment to evaluate a person's giftedness. Obviously this is a human method to give insight into the work of the Spirit, but all the media we have to touch the unseen are human. These tests actually will do more for the individual because they encourage him that he doesn't have to have everything and yet he does have something.

From there take a look at a person's passion. What is it he loves to do? What would he do for free? If he won the lottery, quit his job, and came to work at your church for free, what would he do? Don't get too sidetracked by what people do for a living. Just because he works as a teacher doesn't mean he wants to spend his weekends doing it. Though he may have the spiritual giftedness to work in the elementary department, his heart may beat more for senior adults. If people have the giftedness required (and you do need to determine what gifts are required for each ministry opportunity), place him where he will hate to leave.

Finally, remember that all gifts are equal. The pulpit and the church newsletter have typically been places where only a few gifts are highlighted. We tend to praise the music, the singers, the players, and the speakers, but we often forget the nursery workers, the greeters, the clean up crew, the sound technicians, offering counters, and those who clean the communion trays. If we are going to say that all gifts are equal in the eyes of God, we need to elevate them equally. Bruce Larson says, "Our task as Christians . . . is too live out a style of life that will allow people to discover their worth, their strength, and their uniqueness, and to communicate how much God intends to do with them and for them."[5]

Steve is a young adult who has a huge heart. In every one of his functions he was the guy who found those left out and made them feel special. He would often bring physically or mentally challenged young adults with him to our events and introduce them to people as if he were introducing his parents. Because of this, people were drawn to him. He seemed a natural for a leader with one of our Bible study small groups. So I asked him, begged him, and coerced him, until finally he said "yes." And, just as I suspected, he did a great job as a host for one of these groups. He took care of people, made visitors feel welcome, even made homemade ice cream during the summer. But I could tell this was *not* where his heart was. In fact it wasn't until another ministry area started something called a "Jesus Party" that Steve found his niche. Our minister of family matters created a once-a-month party for kids of all ages who were physically or mentally challenged. They would get a chance to worship, sing, and dance the night away while a leadership team catered to their every need. Steve was a natural for this. None of us had ever seen Steve so passionate about anything he'd ever done. He not only devoted his time, he recruited his friends. And recently Steve helped this team host a "Jesus Prom" so that all of these individuals would be able to wear tuxes or formal dresses and go to

> Steve had the giftedness *and* the passion for this new ministry.

the prom they'd always missed. Steve had the giftedness for leading a small group, but he had the giftedness plus the passion for working with the "Jesus Party." That's the kind of mix we need to look for.

Empower New People, Not Just the Old Guard

The great basketball coach Pat Riley used to say about his use of players during a game, "Play seven, use six, trust only five." Each time I pick up the phone to call and delegate some ministry items I think about this. It is easy for all of us to fall into the trap of only using and trusting a few people. These are the ones who never drop the ball, always get the job done, and always do it well. The problem is that we overuse some to the point of exhaustion, and we cheat others out of getting in the game.

Some of our best leaders sit out in the pews each week, but because we don't know them, or we've never asked them to do anything, their leadership potential remains untapped. A young leader in this postmodern world will find other places to get involved if he senses that the church isn't interested in his contribution. Ever wonder what the church would be like if Jesus had stayed with his parents and brothers and never gone out on a limb to ask guys like Peter, James, and John to join him?

One of the best times to get people plugged into a ministry is right after they are baptized. Granted one of the best ways to baptize people is to get them connected first, but especially after they commit their lives to Christ, they are anxious to know what is next. I often refer them to one or two things to give them a taste of teamwork and ministry. From there we can begin to research giftedness, passion, and ability. Postmoderns will give you one to two chances to plug them in, then they assess that it's not that important to you.

Several weeks ago while introducing one of our ministers to some people at our postmodern service I found myself stating along with everyone's name, "so-and-so was baptized a few weeks ago, and now is a part of a ministry team." You will find that your best billboard for advertisement and recruitment is a satisfied customer.

> Your best billboard for advertisement and recruitment is a satisfied customer.

Create Teachable Moments, Rather Than Damage Control

All of us have felt the pain of criticism. There is nothing like pouring your heart out in a message only to have someone challenge your depth afterwards. It is very frustrating to have someone always complaining about the music while others weep in worship as they experience it. One of the advantages of doing ministry with teams is that it provides a healthy environment in which to place an unhealthy person. When someone complains about the music, ask him or her to come to a programming team meeting and be a part of the spiritual process of charting out a worship experience. When someone complains about a message, ask him or her to join the focus team that helps find the bridges that will connect the gospel with real hurting people. When someone complains about her small group or Sunday school class, ask her to be a part of the team that coordinates everything. When you force someone to look from a different perspective, it forces him or her to develop a new paradigm in their vision.

Once someone is on a team, encourage her leader to reward her progress and success. You can model this by example. Instead of calling your team leaders each week and giving them a list of what they did wrong, sit down with your leaders, tell them what they did right, ask what they are proud of, give them some constructive directives, and reward them with your time and concern. Find other unique ways to encourage them. Using notes, cards, e-mails, gift baskets, and flowers all communicate that you appreciate what they do. Take coffee to their office early in the morning, volunteer to mow their lawn, ask to borrow their car and wash it for them. All of these will give you a platform to provide correction because you have built up investments of encouragement.

Several years ago a young man came to me and asked if he could lead a small group. To be honest, despite all the gifts that he had, I wasn't sure if leading a small group was one of them. But I decided this would be a good teachable moment. We would work through it together, and he would learn along the way. Phil began his small group, and he turned out to be a natural. He appealed to the more intellectual people in our ministry, and each week he provided great insight and encouragement through biblical training. Bruce started going to that small group. He was in a Ph.D. program at the University of Kentucky, and something of this flavor was what he needed. Soon after he got involved, he asked if he could start an apologetics class. Once again I thought, I don't know if this will fly. But, I chose the route of a teachable moment and started to help him promote the class. Bruce had an overwhelming response. People of all ages who had felt the oppression of postmodernity began to connect with this group. One of them was the young adult I mentioned earlier, Rich. Because he had lost his father through his parents' divorce, and had recently lost his mother to leukemia, he was skeptical about everything including the existence of God, but Bruce wouldn't let him go. In fact, he chose to give Rich some responsibility by asking him to help him teach by using Rich's philosophy degree. Rich got involved, reaffirmed his faith, and began to pursue ministry with our staff. The motivation and development with Rich was a long process. He not only let people down along the way, but he became critical about what we were doing. So, rather than just doing damage control every week, I followed the lead of Bruce and asked

Rich to begin leading and teaching more. He was not only a natural, but he became a valuable team player.

I mentioned that mentoring and motivating postmodern leaders is not a quick process. Well, the training of Rich has taken over two years. But because of the faithfulness of Phil, Bruce, and a host of others, Rich organized and held a debate on the campus of the University of Kentucky. He invited students to come and hear two opposing viewpoints on the "Problem of Evil and the Existence of God." He believed, as we all do, that despite living in a world that disregards absolutes, the truth always prevails. He was right, and over 850 students showed up to hear it. Rich is now in full-time ministry. Motivating leaders in a postmodern world is tedious, time consuming, and can even be painful. But in the end, when you stand back and see the ripple that it can create touching hundreds of lives, it is always worth it!

---

[1] Bill Easum, *Postmodernity Lecture* (Louisville, KY: 2000).
[2] Baugh and Hurst, *Getting Real*, p. 48.
[3] Ibid, pp. 46-47.
[4] Matt. 22:37-40.
[5] Bruce Larson, *No Longer Strangers* (Waco: Word. 1971), p. 49.

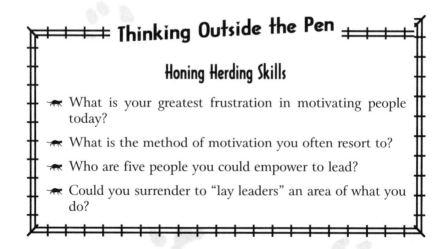

Thinking Outside the Pen

Honing Herding Skills

- What is your greatest frustration in motivating people today?
- What is the method of motivation you often resort to?
- Who are five people you could empower to lead?
- Could you surrender to "lay leaders" an area of what you do?

Top Ten Values of Leaders in a Postmodern World

10

Cat lovers reading this book have given up on seeing anything positive about cats. We apologize for mostly accentuating the negative characteristics of cats to this point. But that was the main point of the book—how herding cats is beyond our grasp as human leaders. We must depend on God to empower us to empower others who exhibit many of the characteristics of cats. Cat lovers would tell you that cats have leadership qualities! Cats have many admirable traits: affection, gentleness, agility, cleanliness, playfulness, and generally more beauty than other animals. We can harness the best in people for the Lord! Granted, we won't need some of the best traits of a cat to be effective church leaders. However it wouldn't hurt.

Oh to live on our own island! I [Rusty] know that I have daydreamed about it. For all of us who have ever wondered what it would be like to be stranded on a desert island, Tom Hanks gave us a movie to help us identify.

Castaway told the story of a man who spent four years on an island. He was forced to live off the land, battle the elements, and walk the tightrope of insanity. Soon after realizing his plight, FedEx packages began to wash ashore from his fallen plane. He opened all but one trying to find survival supplies. Two things were interesting about these packages. One, was the volleyball that he chose to use as a companion, and the other was the package he refused to open to serve as motivation. He wanted to deliver that package one day. Although ministers have the opportunity for better companionship and motivation, they often allow themselves to become shipwrecked on an island.[1]

Every time a minister retreats in his soul and refuses to let others share his life, he heads toward a desert island. Every time a minister sacrifices his heart for the sake of "doing the job," he begins to lose motivation. Every time a minister shoulders the pressure of meeting everyone's needs, he drifts further from the mainland. Every hospital visit or house call that a minister makes because he thinks no one else will allows the water to begin to surround him on all sides. Every time a church leader says, "If it's meant to be, it's up to me," he takes another step closer to complete loneliness.

Besides the obvious shriveling of the minister's soul, there are several other problems with this type of ministry. First, it alienates the church body from being able to serve as fully devoted followers of Christ. Part of being a Christian, and a church member, is to exercise your giftedness so as to serve others. When the minister takes all the responsibility and reserves the menial tasks for the faithful few, he communicates that much of ministry is only accomplished by the ordained. Second, this mentality completely ignores the responsibility of all ministers to equip and train others to lead and do ministry. Ephesians 4:11-12 tells us that "it was he who gave some to be apostles, some to be prophets, some to be evangelists, and some to be pastors and teachers, to prepare God's people for works of service, so that the body of Christ may be built up . . . ." It is not our job to do the ministry by ourselves, but to train others to do it as well. This is usually the by-product of having been taught very little regarding how to train people to do what we do. We can teach the Bible, but we are impotent in training others to teach or lead. Third, while sharing the blame is something we all desire to do, it's not fair to claim all of the praise. One of the attractive things about individualistic ministry is that it allows us to make sure that things are done our way, and then when people enjoy it, we can take the credit. We have to be willing to redirect praise with the same accuracy and enthusiasm as we pass the buck. In a postmodern world that craves authentic leadership, we must resist the urge to rely on our talent and work ethic while we continue to assume that everyone else is just lazy. The greater problem is the deficiency of church leaders who are willing to come alongside people and lead out of genuine character. In the spirit of David Letterman, here are the top ten values that a leader in a postmodern world must possess.

> We can teach the Bible but we are impotent in training others to teach or lead.

1. I will never be satisfied with where I am.

We can never lead people to a place we are not. True, some may reach greater heights than us on their own, but we can never lead them there if we are not already living on that plane. This maxim is true both with spiritual maturity and leadership ability. As leaders of leaders, they will look to us for their direction. It is a rather unsettling concept to realize that the congregation often takes on the personality of its leader.

Jim Collins, author of *Built to Last*, detailed in a business magazine the concept of "mechanisms." He said it's one thing to have goals, but it's another to put into place various mechanisms that enable those goals to be realized.[2] In the end, it is the day-to-day disciplines that turn the athlete into a championship contender. The same is true for a church leader.

We cannot expect to motivate our people to a deeper relationship with Jesus out of mere pep talks and sermons that cheerlead. We must go there ourselves and blaze a trail for others to follow. As a spiritual leader in a postmodern world, we must set the pace for honest investigation of the existence of God, his involvement in our lives, and his direction for the future. People in this culture are asking difficult questions that are not satisfied by our cheap clichés of "the Bible said it, I believe it, and that settles it." They want to know how we can trust a God we cannot see. They want to know personal stories of our ongoing wrestling with the truth and reality of a God that seems to be a casual observer of our pain.

> People are asking difficult questions that are not satisfied with cheap clichés.

The mechanisms to do this are nothing profound, but usually unused. The slow and careful reading of the Bible so as to hear God rather than find a sermon must serve as the lifeline for our understanding of his nature and leading. It is not enough to treat this as we do the taking of our vitamins, a necessary evil we look forward to finishing, but rather the daily conversation with the lover of our soul. Coupled with this comes the mechanism of authentic prayer. Philip Yancey says that he prays while having coffee; after all, this is supposed to be a conversation.[3] The writing down of my prayers, or the praying of Bible prayers help to provide me with a freshness for this experience when I begin to treat it as a shopping list. Often my tendency can be to simply make this another "to do" on my list for the day. Taking a day monthly to be completely alone and "sabbatical" with only God as your conversation partner can help bring life to these experiences. In order to have anything to give other people, I need to allow the gardener of my soul to have large blocks of time for pruning and planting. These mechanisms, along with the other disciplines, provide the framework to keep me progressing in my relationship with God.

Mechanisms are also needed in furthering our leadership ability. Obviously having our heart right with God opens our eyes to see his direction for us and our leaders, but the training and the empowering of people requires us to add new mechanisms to allow us to have something to model. Reading books, attending seminars, interviewing leaders of companies represented in our community, carefully studying the lives of the leaders God used in the Bible, all of these will help replenish your leadership tanks. I have found great encouragement from gleaning insight from my father who managed an assembly line for thirty years. I have recently added to that a mentor who is an elder in our church and is also a leader in the local branch of a global business. The moment I assume I've arrived is the moment I cease to empower others with anything worthwhile.

There are several new cars on the market that have added to the gas-powered engine the ability to be powered by electricity. As you drive, the car will switch over between the two so as to conserve both energy and money.[4] I can tell in my own life when I begin to run out of spiritual empowerment and leadership ability and subsequently switch over to my own resources. When I begin to go with my "gut" rather than prayerful consideration, I am switching tanks to my own ability. When I go into management situations and shoot from the hip, I begin to switch tanks to my own prejudices and feelings rather than proactive and visionary wisdom. Postmodern leaders can see right through this. They know when we are running on empty and when we are supplying them with genuine and godly insight that will help them succeed.

2. I will be real about my relationship with God.

Postmodernity will not tolerate an inauthentic life. Everything about our society screams, "Just tell me the truth!" From the *Survivor* television show to the shock jock Howard Stern, we want honesty. Even the World Wrestling Federation found open arms and increased ratings when they finally came clean by admitting their sport is staged. So how repugnant is it to this culture when the church's leaders pretend that they have walked around God and taken pictures? No matter how much time you spend with God, how many books you read, or how many mountaintop experiences you have had with the Almighty, the truth is we will never have it all figured out. Future leaders in a postmodern culture beg for us to be honest about our struggles so they realize they are not alone.

I was sitting in a classroom in Bible college when I got my first real lesson in this principle. We had been studying the book of Job, and I found myself really wrestling with how God could allow all of these tragedies in Job's life just to win a bet with Satan. While discussing this with some other students, a professor who was no stranger to tragedy entered. He was a modern day Job in all our minds, and also his own. I thought if anyone has the answers, its him. So we began to ask him why God would allow this. He simply answered, "I don't know." Here was a man that was paid to have the answers, but his life experiences caused him to say what we all feel at times: "I don't know."

Here was a man paid to have the answers who still said "I don't know."

I remembered this story years later while sitting in my office counseling a young man new to the faith. He was asking me some very pointed and intense questions as to the reason for pain and for suffering. I had some textbook answers, but I knew he didn't need textbook at that time, he needed empathy. So, I simply looked at him, recounted for him some of my own struggles with faith, and told him, "I don't have a good answer for you. Truth is, I don't know either." As soon as it came out of my mouth I was apprehensive. Did I just disprove what he recently committed his life to? Weeks later he came to me and said that the model I gave him of having faith despite not having all the answers was exactly what he needed to see. When we get really honest with our people and tell them where we are with God, admit our concerns with faith, even be so bold as to talk about some of our temptations, suddenly we become real people with real trust in a God we haven't quite figured out yet.

Joe Boyd, founding pastor of Apex, a church within a church in Las Vegas, tells of his quest for authenticity in what is commonly called "Sin City." In his shame for the mistakes of those who misrepresent the church causing it to be confused with the Bride of Christ, he chose to come clean by not only owning up to the sins of the past, but the sins of the present. He recognized that many people were disgruntled with the obvious hypocrisy in the church, so in order to stress that this was not the type of behavior Jesus commended, he recorded in his journal and later read to his congregation these words of apology:

> **I need to ask forgiveness** for the ongoing corruption of the church at large since the early days of the church, for I believe that it is a sin to use the church for personal or political gain.
>
> **I need to ask forgiveness** for every boring church event, church service, or sermon since the creation of the church, for I believe that it is a sin to bore people with the gospel of Christ.
>
> **I need to ask forgiveness** for the silence of the European church during the Jewish holocaust, and of the American church during the years of slavery,

for I believe that it is a sin for the church of God to sheepishly stand by while innocent people die.

I need to ask forgiveness for the subtle, unspoken belief that we created God in our own image as opposed to embracing our own created-ness, for I believe that it is a sin to deny the power, mystery, and miracle that is God.

I need to ask forgiveness for the weight of legalism that has shackled the church, making it oppressively boring and guilt-centered, for I believe that it is a sin to deny people their freedom in Christ.

I need to ask forgiveness for every right wing political zealot who has ever advocated violence against innocent people in the name of Christ, for I believe that it is a sin to judge in the place of God.

I need to ask forgiveness for every sidewalk and soap-box preacher who has so much as cracked open a Bible with anger or pride in his heart, for I believe that it is a sin to misrepresent the character of a loving God.

I need to ask forgiveness for every cult leader and extremist group leader who has ever led people astray in the name of Christ, for I believe that it is a sin to desire the position of Jesus as the head of the church.

I need to ask forgiveness for every preacher who has thought with his zipper, or his wallet, or his ego, for I believe that it is a sin to lead the church while consumed with unconfessed sin.

I need to ask forgiveness for the millions of men in the church who have somehow stretched the Word of God to validate their own sexist views, for I believe that it is a sin to dishonor a woman.

I need to ask forgiveness for the thousands of church splits and denominational factions that have ripped the body of Christ in every direction except heavenward, for I believe that it is a sin to bring disunity to the body of Christ.

I need to ask forgiveness for the thousands of churches who are set up as extravagant social clubs, for I believe that it is a sin to ignore the poor and hurting among you.

I need to ask forgiveness for every misspent dime that was ever placed in an offering basket, for I believe that it is a sin to waste an old lady's tithe.

I need to ask forgiveness for the prostituting of the American church and the American minister to the American dream, for I believe that it is a sin for the church or her leaders to love money more than God.

I need to ask forgiveness for every self-centered, self-proclaimed "miracle worker" who has sold people counterfeit hope and light and fluffy theology for $19.95 plus shipping and handling, for I believe that it is a sin to spit in the face of God.

I need to ask forgiveness for every pastor or teacher who has ever stepped in front of his congregation without preparing or praying or confessing his sin, for I believe that the sin of the leader somehow mysteriously thwarts the growth of the local church.

I need to ask forgiveness for every sin of every priest, pastor, minister, reverend, teacher, elder, deacon, pope, nun, monk, missionary, Sunday school teacher, worship leader, apostle, prophet, and church member from Pentecost until this very second, for I believe that sin is the problem with the church.

And lastly for me. For my sin—my pride, my lust, my anger, my laziness, my lack of faith, my lack of mercy, my overanalysis of life, my immaturity, my filthy decrepit heart that is bent to evil, forgive me, if you can, for I am a sinner. Blame me and others like me for a messed up church that has done more than its share of evil deeds. Blame me if you have to, but don't blame the Bride of Christ whom I love. The church is perfect. Perfect in theory, perfect in origin and sometimes even perfect in practice. Our sin corrupts her, but she never folds. Our pride limits her growth, but she never dies. For she is the Bride of Christ—perfect before him. She is the Body of Christ—his hands, his feet, his voice. And she is the Hope of the World.[5]

3. I will cast a vision.

Postmodern leaders are not attracted to maintenance. Issuing a call for people to come and help you plug holes in the proverbial dam is not appealing for them. They not only want to make a difference, they want to do it through the completing of a vision. For many, the vision will need to come from the church leader.

Several years ago, our leadership team in the young adult ministry spent a considerable amount of time casting the vision for new and exciting ways to connect the lost people of our culture with Jesus. A leader in our college ministry caught a glimpse of this vision and put hands and feet on it. He suggested we do "church" for college students one Sunday morning down on campus. Another leader took that idea a little further and suggested the use of an old theater within walking distance. Some other leaders began the promotion, and before long we were set to go. I can remember standing outside of this theater watching hundreds of students making their way inside. One leader then whispered to me, "If you build it, they will come!"

If you build it, they will come.

Not long after that, some of our post-college people took that idea and began to tailor it to reach the young professionals of our city. We batted around several venues until someone finally had the guts to say, "How about a bar?" After a few moments of deciding whether or not my employment at our church was something I wanted to keep, I chose to throw caution to the wind and said, "Sounds great!" So, one Monday night we rented out a bar, promoted it everywhere, brought in a local band, and watched as hundreds crammed into that establishment to do church.

The leaders who participated in this mission talked about it for months. This kind of involvement never would have happened if we had called them to do church as usual. Risk-taking is always appealing. No one ever skydives out of a plane or rappels off a mountain alone.

4. I will encourage unique giftedness and style.

It has taken us many years to recognize that people really do have different spiritual gifts and passions, and that putting them to use requires unique methods of implementation. But the other facet of leadership in the church that we often overlook is that people have different leadership styles. God has wired us up in such a way that not only do most of us not have the same spiritual giftedness as Billy Graham, but not all of us lead like General Patton.

Bill Hybels, in an audiotape series on church leadership, lists for us a variety of different leadership styles. He mentions that just as much as there are visionary leaders who can see the next hill we need to climb, there are also directional and strategic leaders who can tell us how to get there. He explains that there are some managerial leaders who like to keep things moving in the right direction, and there are entrepreneurial leaders who aren't satisfied unless they are starting something new. A healthy understanding that people will not always lead the way you do promotes the enabling of leaders who not only differ from you, but can fill in the gaps of your leadership weaknesses.[6]

Worship leaders are prime examples of this. Typically the preaching minister of the church can take on more of a visionary or strategic style of leadership. His giftedness lies in his ability to teach and lead. Often the worship leader is just the opposite. Artists tend to be more relational and shepherding in their style of leadership, while their gifts lie in their musical talent and prayerful ability to lead music. Forcing these types of leaders to direct only in the manner you choose stifles their natural style. The essentials of authentically loving God and people need to be maintained, but the failure to allow worship leaders to do so in their own unique fashion will cause unwanted tension between the two most visible leaders on your staff.

5. I will be more concerned about people's souls than their work.

Sometimes in the interest of training and empowering leaders tunnel vision can set in. We can become so obsessed with getting the job done that we neglect the soul of the leader. There will be times that empowering people who we know will drop the ball will not necessarily hurt anyone, but only build trust into that person.

There have been several people in our ministry that have promised great things, asked for responsibility, and when given it never produced fruit. They constantly take up your time in training and mentoring, but in the end the job never gets done. In a postmodern culture many of these types of leaders have no knowledge of their giftedness, style, or passion, they simply need to be close to you in order to find the strength to keep going.

> **Walking alongside a below-average leader raises esteem while modeling real leadership**

Your greatest challenge with these types of leaders is to read between the lines. Understand that though you may not have an extra hour for a person who has done nothing for you lately, her soul may desperately need it. Walking alongside a leader who constantly performs below average will cause her to find a new esteem in leadership while learning from you what a leader truly is. From here you can begin to build upon that time invested by helping her discover her giftedness, style, and how to succeed.

Because this is such a tedious process, your reinventing of yourself is mandatory. You cannot provide this type of individual attention with everyone you lead. There must be other leaders you have built into that understand this concept and are willing to mentor young leaders with no history of success into future leaders with great potential.

6. I will stay relevant.

Many of us go through transitions in churches in order to connect with a new culture. For some, it is very difficult because we do not enjoy the new methods, but for others it fits like a glove. We have recently started an additional service at our church that targets the postmodern mind-set. I get the pleasure not only of teaching at it often, but also helping with the programming of this service. It just so happens that this new style of worship fits my tastes perfectly. But I also have begun to notice that if I am not careful, I can begin crafting services around what I would enjoy. It occurred to me recently that, as much as I enjoy our service now, one day we will have to transition to a new style that I may not. Will I be as motivated by the unconnected at that point that I will surrender my programming pen to those who see things from a more culturally relevant perspective than I do? In his book, *The Leadership Engine*, Noel Tichey comments on this type of willingness to change. He writes, ". . . winning leaders are masters of transitions. They are people who relish change. They personally draw energy from transitions, and using transitions to create productive energy in others is one of their most powerful tools as leaders."[7]

One mechanism that will help is constantly pulling in new thinkers into the idea process of the crafting of our services. This keeps our worship leader and myself from constantly providing our "greatest hits" each week.

This is true from both corporate and individual standpoints. I must continue to keep my finger on the pulse of society so I know the means to communicate the gospel. I can discover what their struggles are by observing the bestseller lists at bookstores. I can hear what their questions are by listening to popular music. I can observe the latest views on government, religion, and society by noticing what television and the cinema are producing. And nothing substitutes for spending large amounts of time in local coffeehouses and diners where the people of your town gather. Knowing your people and the culture they live in will help you connect rather than miss the mark when you lead from the pulpit or lead your staff meeting on a weekly basis.

> Knowing your people will help you connect rather than miss the mark.

7. I will stress excellence more than perfection.

One typical, yet unsatisfactory, method of leadership is to lead through correction. It is easy to begin to assume that by identifying the problems and taking proper action, then one can achieve perfection. The problem with this style is that it implies that perfection is the only desired result. While there is benefit in constructive criticism, postmodern leaders will become easily frustrated if they are constantly corrected. Setting excellence as the goal will allow you to have the standard for how you execute your ministry without assuming that perfection is expected. I find it easy to evaluate church services, special programs, or service projects with a clipboard in hand. Searching for perfection can be a tedious and never-ending challenge that will rob you and your leaders of the satisfaction of doing the Lord's work.

I've caught myself on more than one occasion failing to completely release a task to someone and instead going behind him to alter his work in order to achieve perfection. It's not that he doesn't do the job with excellence, it's just that

I have something else in mind. But when I state by my words or my actions that excellence isn't enough, but rather perfection is the only thing acceptable, I devalue the work and creativity of these leaders. Hans Finzel writes in *The Top Ten Mistakes Leaders Make* that one of the deadly mistakes we struggle with is "dirty delegation." Of the many reasons for this, he cites "the fear of losing authority and the fear of the work being done poorly" as our downfall in completely surrendering a task.[8]

In seeking to avoid a perfection-driven controlling nature, standards of excellence must be clearly stated up front. First, define for your leaders what success looks like. Identify the two to three things that will be the result of a job well done. Second, allow the person to know the attitude that needs to be possessed in accomplishing the task. This will help communicate that there is more to this than simply completion; the Spirit of Christ must be exhibited. Third, state clearly your expectations for their recruiting of team members. Let them know that they will not be doing this alone. Finally, give your team a timeline. Once they agree to the job, let them know when it begins and then when it ends. All of these standards will serve as mechanisms to evaluate team excellence without settling into the never ending critiquing of task perfection.

8. I will model grace rather than legalism.

Most postmodern leaders have a fear that if they make one false move, they will be removed. They feel that church leaders will not tolerate their volunteers having any flaws, and if any are exposed, their trustworthiness is tarnished forever. Dealing with sin in the camp is a great way to model grace and forgiveness. I'm not saying that we ignore it or sweep everything under the rug; these issues should be dealt

> They have a fear of being removed for one error.

with. But they should be addressed in private, and then the person needs to be affirmed in public. If it is a matter of substantial implications, a sabbatical from leadership coupled with care and accountability can help restore a leader to his or her position. In each of these situations, people are watching to see how these types of matters are handled from the church's perspective—with grace and accountability or with harsh legalism.

Once on a college retreat one of our sponsors had such a teachable moment. This sponsor, Woody, was new to our team and had only been a Christian for a couple of years. His difficult past and fresh enthusiasm about God's grace were encouraging both to our students and to me. Things had been going very well the entire weekend until we loaded up in the vans and headed out to play paint ball. Soon after our trip began, Woody, who was driving a van full of students had to make a series of difficult maneuvers to keep up. He was getting frustrated and it didn't help when he accidentally cut somebody off. The offended driver cast a rather vengeful look towards their van, and Woody responded like he would have two years ago—with a well-crafted phrase complete with a carefully placed cuss word. The silence lasted for only a couple of seconds, though it seemed to be an eternity for Woody. The entire van then erupted in laughter. He apologized to the van, we spoke in private later, and that was it. He continued to be visible in ministry tasks. The grace and forgiveness extended to him by all not only restored a leader who blossomed into a dedicated man of God, but also encouraged the entire van that everyone is not only in process here, but is welcome as well.

9. I will recognize that just because it's not my idea, doesn't mean it's a bad idea.

Often leaders get so focused on what they hope to achieve or the vision that they have that they assume that anyone with another idea is off course. The truth is, God can use many different ideas and still maintain the same momentum toward the same goal. If our goal is clear and the values we have are known, then the idea process has its playing field.

We must be prepared for people of this culture to constantly have ideas. With all of the daily forms of communication, there are massive amounts of data going into our minds that can foster a variety of concepts. We used to refer to one of our leaders as "forty per minute" because that's how many ideas he could throw out for just about any topic. Our difficulty with this stems from our fear that if the idea is not ours, the ship may get away from us. The trick for a coach of leaders is to not jump on or off every bandwagon.

Most postmodern leaders with visionary leadership simply want to be heard, and then that is it; they are off to the next idea. So don't restructure your ministry over every idea. If it is truly from God and has staying power, it will return and be championed by others. After hearing an idea, I often tell the vision caster to pray and journal about the idea for a few weeks and see where God takes it. If he returns with more passion, I ask if anyone else can help him form a team to blaze this trail. We never want to encourage people to work on their own, but rather with a community. Finally, if he finds a team and has a plan, then we do all we can from a resource, publications, and direction perspective to help the plan succeed.

Church leaders in this empowering process must remember that many great ideas might not be their own and that should not limit their support. We had a long-running young adult Bible study that I felt had run its course. God took us in another direction, and we shut the Bible study down. The new concept was a tremendous blessing and things were building momentum when a team of the young adult Bible study leaders approached me and said they wanted to bring it back. I was skeptical at first. This might detract from our new vision, it might be a huge flop and leave this team defeated, or it might not be operated with the same care as before. But I chose to trust them and this process. They prayed about it, they built a team, we helped them cover some bases, and they started it. It was and still is a fantastic success. Just because it wasn't my idea, doesn't mean that it wouldn't work.

Just because it wasn't my idea doesn't mean it wouldn't work.

This is the same process that many of our ministries in the church have taken on their way to great blessings. From our inner-city youth work to a group of people who take their pets to nursing homes to encourage the elderly, no matter how undoable the idea is for me personally, that doesn't mean that it shouldn't be done. Leadership in this culture requires that we encourage others to think outside the box.

10. I will pray that my leaders will do greater things than I have.

One of the toughest hills to descend from as a leader is that of self-glorification. So much of ministry can be based on peoples' perceptions. When we go out of our way to benefit someone, the temptation to ask, "How will this make me look good?" is the forbidden fruit we often admire. It is the allure of ministry to prepare and produce in such a way so as to impress or astound others with our brilliance, our depth, or our ability. True leadership is just the opposite of this.

Over the past fifty years we have mainly attributed the leadership tag to those who take the hill, motivate people on the way, and demand respect out of their followers. The picture of the Son of God with a towel and a wash basin quickly fades from our minds. But in a culture of postmodernity that is starving for authenticity and empowerment, servant leadership has never been more needed. Reading our resume to postmodern leaders won't command respect, but sacrificing our own agenda will stand out like a medal of honor. Telling a young adult that you are in charge here will not cause someone to want to fall in line, but not being afraid to help take out the trash or clean the bathrooms will be like wearing a shirt that says "CEO." As a result, when you begin to let servant leadership take the forefront of your agenda, you will then need to rappel from the lofty heights of the pursuit of acclaim.

First and Second Samuel record how Samuel had to come to grips with the fact that David would not only be a great leader, but he would be greater than Samuel. History would remember King David more often than Judge Samuel. Samuel had to wrestle with this truth, as did Saul. Samuel was content to see David assume that leadership notoriety, but Saul was not. Saul was consumed with jealousy, degrading comments, and attempts at murder. Saying "God bless" to those going up the ladder, as we appear to be going down it, is never an easy task.

We must not only allow someone to become a greater leader than us, we must seek him out and propel him to this status. A preacher must never suppress the talent of his youth minister for fear his congregation might enjoy the youth minister more. A worship leader must never deny solos and worship leading experience to a gifted lay leader for fear that someone might like her voice more. Leaders who leave a lasting impact, especially in this postmodern world, do so by ensuring that a greater leader comes behind them.

We hired a worship leader for our postmodern-targeted events and service a few years ago. Tom is a very gifted and well-respected singer, songwriter, and worship leader, but when he arrived, he was very raw in his leadership development. Over the past three years we have watched as he has taken on a very coachable spirit. He listens to criticism, he responds and doesn't react to difficulties, and he is passionate about developing his skills. His leadership style is different than mine. I marvel as I watch him lead his worship teams with a style of encouragement and relaxation. I am astounded by his incredible ability to mentor and train young talent. And I am constantly blessed by the times that he leads worship and I don't even notice him. As a result, his leaders are drawn to him, his band respects him, and the fellow worshipers follow his lead. The truth is, he has become such an amazing leader at what he does that I could stand up and read the phone book after he has led us in worship and the people would still leave blessed and challenged. It occurred to me one day that I would be honored to call him my "David"; I only pray that I don't become his "Saul."

> I could stand up and read the phone book and people would still leave blessed.

Leadership in a postmodern world is somewhat of a paradox. It requires the complete surrender of self while constantly seeking out where God is leading you. It verifies that you can't lead people past where you are, but some day others will move beyond you. It states that we don't understand the old so we want the new, but after a while the use of the old is considered beneficial. It says, whatever techniques you use, they had better be fresh, and don't get too satisfied with them because just because they worked yesterday, it doesn't mean they will work tomorrow. It says, "I want to remain anonymous," but then it begs to be recognized. And it cries out for meaning, but then states that it doesn't care.

I think about the two men on their way toward Emmaus.[9] I'm not sure what was there, or why they were going, but I do know what they were leaving. They were walking away from the memories of future plans that had now faded, a political renaissance that had now disintegrated, and a visionary leader who was now gone. They were leaving the site of their problems, but still had their problems. That is postmodernity.

We are encountering a mass exodus of people that are leaving the site of their problems. They are fleeing from the hope of career advancement in a field in which they received their degree. They are walking away from the trust in authority that their broken home and corrupt government stole from them. And they are running away from the belief that someone can actually heal their soul and give them meaning in life. But nonetheless, they still maintain the very pain they think they are leaving. They walk toward a sedative for life in escapism while all along they need the companionship of Jesus.

That's the trouble with herding cats! You're never sure what direction they will head next, even though you know where they need to be. God, give us the grace and direction to lead those who crave to be lead, yet resist leading.

---

[1] *Castaway*, Fox Productions, 2000.

[2] Jim Collins, "What Comes Next?" *Inc. Magazine* (October, 1997).

[3] Philip Yancey, *Reaching for the Invisible God* (Grand Rapids, Zondervan. 2000), p. 203.

[4] "Combustionbuster," *Lexington Herald-Leader* (December 18, 2000).

[5] Joe Boyd, "The Apex Story," as told to me for this publication, 2001.

[6] Bill Hybels, *Leveraging Your Leadership Style*, Audiotape, Willow Creek Resources, 1997.

[7] Noel M. Tichey, *The Leadership Engine* (New York: Harper Collins, 1997), p. 150.

[8] Hans Finzel, *The Top Ten Mistakes a Leader Makes* (Wheaton: Victor Books. 1994), p. 100.

[9] Luke 24:13-35.

Thinking Outside the Pen

Honing Herding Skills

🐾 What are your spiritual gifts, passion, and leadership style?

🐾 Do you struggle with relinquishing control?

🐾 Do your program leaders understand clearly what is expected of them so they can take charge of their task and run with it?

Stories of Swimming Techniques–Within the Church Pool

11

Every once in a while I [Jeff] will read a story in someone's book that is so unbelievable, so inconceivably outrageous, I will think to myself, "They had to have made that up." You are about to hear such a story, and it is true. I was sitting in my office one day when I heard some noise outside in the hallway. I didn't pay much attention to it, but soon one of the other ministers came bursting into my office. He told me that there was a naked man running around in our building. Now you have to understand that the tenor of our office is such that we often play practical jokes on each other. I thought this was a bit overboard, but I was willing to play along and so I stood there with him, smiling, waiting for the punch line. He didn't return the smile and there was no punch line. There was only a naked man, running loose in our building.

There are situations in ministry for which our formal training prepares us. Weddings, funerals, counseling, and sermon preparation are the traditional situations. Ministering to estranged, naked people was not covered in normal practical ministry classes. The other minister and I set out down the hallway in search of this naked man. Someone pointed us in the direction of the sanctuary. As we approached the dark worship center, my mind was racing with the possible scenarios that we would find upon opening the door and honestly, truthfully, I didn't want to go in to see which scenario would play itself out. I slowly opened the door to the room. It was a weekday and the lights were out. There is quite a distance between the main entrance doors to the sanctuary and the stage, so I peered in quietly, not knowing what would happen next in the empty room. I spoke, "Is anyone in here?" There was no response. "Hello?" I asked, hoping that there would be no response and at the same time wanting to find this man. Then I heard a gasp for air and the sound of water. There on the stage I saw a head emerge from the baptistery and heard a deep breath drawn and then immediately, the unknown head plunged back down under the water. The other minister and I rushed into the back room to the baptistery doors and up the stairs to the water where we found one naked man in the bottom of the tank.

What next? Here in our church, in our quiet, serene place of worship, a young man had entered with an agenda. (We found out later that he believed he was told by God to find some Holy water and to drown himself in it). He felt this was the only way that he could deal with his sin and be washed clean. Whatever his warped sense of redemption was, he had selected our place of worship to carry out his agenda, and he had wedged himself in the bottom of the tank and was not coming out. I stood on one side of the steps, two other ministers stood on the other side and we looked at each other and the man and thought almost out loud, "What do we do?"

"What do we do next?" That would be a good question for all of us to ask at this point in our discussion of ministry in a changing paradigm with a changing culture. We stand at the water's edge of ministry in a new millennium. It is different from anything we have ever seen or known before, and yet we have generations of people who are drowning themselves in the rough and angry water of life and have nowhere to turn. What will we do? How will we respond?

"What do we do next" is a good question for all of us in considering the changing culture.

I had a couple of options in my situation. I could have just walked away. I could have waited for the police to come or for him to drown. Either way, the option of noninvolvement was a real possibility. I wouldn't have to ruin my watch or my clothes. There would have been no physical discomfort to me at all. In fact, I could have easily justified noninvolvement. He could have been a danger to me. If I would have stepped in the water, he could have tried to drown me instead. Not getting involved would have been the cleanest, easiest option in many ways. In many ways, this has also been the chosen course of action for the church.

I could have also taken another route. I could have walked back down the stairs, taken my shoes and socks off, my pants, my watch, my jewelry, and everything that had value. I could have put on a pair of waders and then made my way back to the man and climbed in to fish him out. After all, didn't Jesus say that he would make us fishers of men? This tactic would have been more engaging than the first, but by the time I returned, ready for the task, he might have finished what he had started.

My final option was to jump in and help pull him to safety. To offer whatever I could to someone in a desperate point in his life. As we stood there, in that split second, someone said, "Grab his leg and pull him up." I stepped down into the water and began to pull this boy to the surface. Each time I would get him up, he would struggle to get back down to the bottom of the tank. Finally, after minutes of struggling, we were able to pull him to safety on the stage. I ruined a watch, some shoes, and my wallet; but this boy's life was now his to live again.

We are standing on the edge of a cultural shift. People are dying all around us and we have what they desperately need. Sacrifices will have to be made. Our comfortable ministry forms will have to be evaluated and possibly shattered and replaced with new and sometimes uncomfortable forms. We will have to give up something that may be valuable to us as church leaders. But our options are few. We can walk away and let them drown. We can take our time and prepare ourselves for a battle that may pass us by when we finally feel comfortable. Or we can jump in and get wet. The five stories in chapters 11 and 12 are a collection of techniques and methods used for swimming in this new paradigm. Granted, cookie-cutter processes are no longer available, but there may be some things that you can transplant to help push your ministry into the deep end.

What you will see are five different ways to do this type of ministry. Two are representative of ministries within churches. The first is a *Sub-Ministry* for postmoderns in an existing congregation. Much like we see youth ministry, many young adult ministries will provide something in addition to the main worship service at their church. This is designed to strengthen the connection of young adults, and provide a first step for people to bring their friends to. The second is a *Postmodern Service*. This is a church that simply started an additional service and targeted a different postmodern audience.

In chapter 12, the remaining three stories portray ministries apart from the traditional church system. The third story is a *Church-within-a-Church* (CWIC). It is an existing church that allows a young adult ministry to form into a church and then transition into their own entity complete with various ministries offered (small groups, children, etc.) and even eldership. The fourth is a *Church-within-a-Church Plant.* This is a CWIC that moves out with the help of its originating congregation and plants itself as a new church somewhere else in the community. And the final story is from a *Postmodern Church Planting Organization* that seeks to rid church plants of the hindrances that promote failure while creating teams and providing resources to do postmodern ministry.

> ## STORY ONE—THE VINE
> ## A Sub-Ministry of Southeast Christian Church
> ## Louisville, Kentucky
> ### Richard Mosqueda, College Minister

In 1994 I arrived at Southeast Christian Church as an intern for the high school department. The college ministry at the time was an effective Sunday morning class taught by Dave Stone. Yet after Dave switched ministry positions and was no longer able to teach the class, people started leaving the class. The class got so small that it was canceled. The church then tried to launch a program on Tuesday nights, which only had about thirty people regularly attending. This, too, was canceled, and the Sunday morning program resumed. Again, after a depressing turnout, the class terminated.

This was beginning to be a big problem for Southeast. We had a great youth ministry and young adult ministry, each with thriving Sunday morning classes and many other activities. Yet there seemed to be a gaping hole during the college years. We were losing most of our students in the transition from high school to college. We were finally able to pinpoint this loss to two areas.

The most obvious reason for our loss of students can be found in their choice of colleges. Most of our graduating high school students at Southeast go out of the area for college. We only get those out-of-Louisville students then for three to four months out of the year—when they are home for vacations. Our actual numbers each week during the summer are even lower though due to mission trips, internships, and vacations.

The other factor in our declining numbers has been simply the difficulty of the transition from the youth ministry atmosphere to the college ministry atmosphere. Our high school students have been in the same school systems for years, which means they are familiar with the other students and are comfortable with their groups of friends. They have also been going to church for a significant amount of time, which means they are familiar with the youth ministry and its leaders. Our youth leaders have played a big part in their major decisions throughout high school. When graduation arrives, their friends go in every direction, they are no longer invited to the youth programs, and they are forced to start all over in another ministry.

Too many students have a hard time because they expect to find the same warm feeling that their youth programs had. They don't realize that it took years for that feeling to form. This loss of a sense of familiarity coupled with newfound freedom and a desire to experience college life proves to be too much to handle. The transition overwhelms the students.

That is why the college ministry tries to build relationships with the students while they are in high school. We are still working on ways to get them involved now so they stay involved after they leave high school. I would say many churches across the nation are facing the same dilemma. Statistics indicate that 85% of all graduating seniors will drop out of church in their first year of college.

So in an effort to turn the tide during these crucial years in a college student's life, one of the first things I established was a Sunday morning class. We ran into some problems right from the beginning. The first problem was the classroom setting. I can't think of a worse setting to teach this generation. There are too many things that say "lecture" and "keep quiet." We also struggled with the teaching material. We could not establish a common goal for the class because we had regulars who wanted to go deeper, but we also had visitors who seemed to choke on the deep teachings. Despite these obstacles and my lack of knowledge, our small class began to grow.

I started spending time going out to eat with our college students and asking them a plethora of questions. I asked them to tell me some of their biggest needs. I asked students what they thought of church and Christians. The responses I got were that church is boring and irrelevant and that Christians are hypocrites. With these responses in mind, I set off to create a program that would be real, relevant, and relational. I recruited some of my sharpest students and started praying and planning. We came up with a program called *The Grounds*. It was designed to have a coffeehouse atmosphere. We had couches, tables covered with white paper, crayons to draw with, candles, and Christmas lights.

The Grounds provided a program that was new and different for us. The first hour of each evening was spent listening to a band playing cover tunes related to a certain theme. We provided discussion questions at the tables so people could interact with each other. We included video clips and a devotional message or lesson that brought everything together. We usually brought in another band to play during the second hour. Even after the two-hour program, people would still hang out for another hour. *The Grounds* was very much a relational program. We had provided some intense teaching, but its main goal was to build relationships.

One of my goals for each evening was that our leaders would be able to sit with visitors and get to know them on a one-on-one basis. This very personal approach would allow the visitors to ask questions about God that a large group format would not allow. As a result of this very personal attention, most of the time we had to kick people out instead of trying to get them to stay. Teaching for two hours would be a hard sell. But if you mix up the teaching with other activities and make it effective, time will not matter.

Because we are encountering a generation that doesn't know how to build relationships, we have tried to create opportunities for people to get to know each other. The students that attend our programs want to meet people, otherwise they wouldn't be there. The problem is just that they are scared to do it. One of the things that I was seeing was that many of the people in this generation were just floating by and that real involvement required an invitation from peers. I learned this lesson when I started doing small groups. I went out and recruited great adult leaders, and I gave each adult leader a few student leaders. I soon found out that my student leaders weren't showing up to Bible studies and the group remained relatively small. The next semester I tried something different. I gave the Bible study to the student leaders. I told them they were going to teach and recruit people for their Bible study. The adult leaders would simply host the Bible study and help build relationships. It was amazing. Each group doubled and even tripled just by giving them the freedom to run with it. Be prepared to be amazed when you allow your students to run with ministry.

The Vine is an evolution of *The Grounds* with a focus on worship. The name is derived from Jesus' words in John 15. We wanted to create a worship service that acknowledged that we can't do a thing without Christ. *The Vine* is an intense worship service. Our goal is to connect with God. We meet on Sunday nights at 6:30 p.m. Sunday night is a great night because there isn't a lot going on. The people that come to Sunday morning services are the people that have been coming to church for quite some time. We have found that having only Sunday morning services will discourage visitors and hurt a ministry.

The Vine has been the biggest way that I have seen God move since I have been doing ministry. It is a worship service that consists of intense worship (45-60 minutes), intense teaching (30 minutes), and communion (15 minutes). One of the biggest differences in our service is our concept of worship. In most churches (even our main worship services), we start off with a song service followed by a sermon. The announcements are made and everyone is dismissed. If we were to compare this to football, it is almost as if we let the Holy Spirit (worship time) get the team to the 20 and then we expect the preacher to take it in for the touchdown. Even if the preacher preaches a really convicting message, the people who attend don't have time to reflect because they are out in the parking lot within five minutes of the sermon. What we do (*Vine* service and high school ministry) is start off with worship and then have our teaching time in the middle. We follow that up with more worship, but during this time, we give people permission to go to our garden. (We built a prayer garden in our auditorium that contains trees, shrubs, and a water fountain.) There they may take communion, or just sit and meditate on what God is saying to them. This segment is more reflective in nature. By setting aside this time at the end of the service, we want the Holy Spirit to score the touchdown. It is amazing how God uses that time to touch the hearts of the people at *The Vine.*

A few closing points: First, in regard to how *The Vine* fits into the church's mission. The church made some strategic goals for the college ministry and one of the main priorities was to create a service that is reaching this generation. This service is not considered one of our main worship services but is an option for people in the church. Second, atmosphere and experience play a major part in attracting this generation. If you meet in a room that has a cold feel to it, you have already lost the battle. Students are no longer looking for programs. They are looking for experiences that go past sharing information. They have to *feel* it. They have to be able to use their senses. And finally, keep in mind that many students no longer have loyalty. They will go to a Bible study at one church, outreach events at another, and special events at another, which makes it harder for students to build community and get plugged in. Don't let this diffuse your passion to help them see Christ. God is always faithful in our small efforts to further his work with this generation.

STORY TWO—608
The Postmodern Service of Southland Christian Church
Lexington, Kentucky
T.D. Oakes, Worship Leader

It would be difficult to trace exactly when or where the original seeds for the "608" began. I guess we would point to a spirit of worship that we began to experience through our work with the young adult ministry at Southland. Through our weekend and midweek college age and young adult ministry programs we began to try to create a worship environment that would allow young adults to experience God in a very real and powerful way.

Our idea was to remove obstacles that would come in the way of an authentic, real, and relevant time of interaction with God and each other. To achieve this we created a comfortable environment and an engaging program. Instead of a traditionally formatted program we would continually try to be creative with the interplay of praise, message, testimony, and the other elements. The message would be related primarily with the use of story. The praise time was focused on drawing people closer into the heart of God, to a place of intimacy where God could really work on people's hearts. We truly sensed that the generations we were now dealing with wanted worship. Whether or not they always sang, they wanted to see what it looked like for people to interact with God. The more we began to refine this format of worship the more we began to see the effects it was having on our young adults.

It was also becoming more evident that many of the changes we were making were significantly different from the format of the weekend services of Southland at the time. Southland had five services simply hitting the ball out of the park, but we knew that despite the fact that our attendance was in the thousands, we also recognized that there were still thousands who weren't there. The leadership at Southland wanted to be sensitive to those who might connect in a different way than what we were offering. For instance, we were discovering that while the seekers from previous generations tended to connect best with less music and more drama and sermon, the postmodern generations appeared to desire more worship and music with less speaking. They also seemed to crave interaction. Our first five services were constrained due to time issues, but another service at another time might be able to provide more community through interaction, through question and answer time with the speaker, group communion, testimonies from the baptistery, and a dialogical message. The culture in Lexington for many postmodern people lends itself to heavy Saturday night activity, lazy Sunday mornings, and nothing to do on Sunday night. So, we thought Sunday night might be our best bet to pull off this type of service. Not youth group, not a single's mixer, not a traditional Sunday night service, but a sixth service. In fact, our tag phrase was "Same . . . but different." Recognizing these differences and seeing the potential through the success we were having I believe were the first seeds for the 608 service.

Another major seed was our experience with an on-campus college worship service that utilized what we had been learning. Once a semester we would either rent a theater by campus, or reserve an auditorium on campus and hold a Sunday worship service. The response was unbelievable! We would have double, or sometimes triple the amount of people that normally came to our Sunday morning college program. This type of response signaled to us that there was a whole group of people in our community who were responding to this type of worship experience. We knew that a huge opportunity existed to influence even more people, and that possibly the only way to reach them was through a different type of worship environment.

Through these experiences Rusty George and I would always end up talking about what it would be like to have a service that would allow this same type of worship experience. Finally, Rusty approached our senior minister Mike Breaux about the idea. The amazing thing is that Breaux had been thinking some of the same things. He encouraged Rusty to begin the process of planning for this new service.

Throughout the process of planning and then doing the

608 service, Breaux's support, wisdom, and leadership have been essential. It was actually his idea to signify that this type of service would be a "little different" by giving it an odd starting time . . . 6:08. Since we refer to all of our other services by their times, this one would be no different. The benefit of having the senior minister completely behind the service allowed us to step out in confidence. But his support did not stop with just a rubber-stamped O K. He wanted to be involved. He stressed something we had already been sensing and that was to make this new service the *sixth* weekend service of Southland, not a church within a church, or college/young adult service. The church within a church model is a great model, but we knew it wasn't the best scenario for us. So we did whatever was necessary to make sure that this was the "same . . . but different." The sermon series, topic, title, and text would be the same for this new sixth service as the other five services, yet because 75% of the time someone else would teach the 608, the approach would usually be a little different.

We asked if Breaux would be willing to teach at least 25% of the time, if not more. He is a brilliant communicator and crosses all generational lines. Not only would his teaching reach this audience, but it would also be important for the attendees of this service to know they were just as much a part of Southland as the other services, and his presence would communicate that. He was more than willing to be involved. This kind of support added a sense of legitimacy to the new service. Throughout the process Breaux's wisdom, ideas, and support have been invaluable to the 608's success. It did so much for our people to either hear the senior minister teaching and answering their questions at this service, or to look across the aisle and see him worshiping with them.

However, although supportive and willing to submit ideas Breaux did not try to control the way the new service would look. Instead he entrusted our team to develop a service that would reach a new target of people that perhaps did not connect to the other five services. That is incredible leadership on Breaux's part. He recognized that he had valuable insight to give to the service. But he didn't try to control it.

The planning process for the 608 involved our putting together a team of young adults who would help us shape the way this service would look and feel. Outside of the hand of God first and foremost, followed by the support of our senior minister, nothing can surpass the valuable contribution given by our volunteers. From the beginning they were the ones who organized greeters, set-up and tear-down teams, arts and atmosphere efforts, video and music contributions, programming and worship development, and all of the technical aspects of running the lights and sound.

We also tried to do our homework before we launched. We did several formal and informal surveys of young adults in the community to see what the needs were. Most of the feedback we were receiving was emphasizing what we had been experiencing all along. People were looking for authenticity; they were looking to really experience God through worship, as well as find real community with others.

Based on the responses we were getting and the things that we had learned, our team began to develop what would become the 608. The things we wanted to focus on were just that: authenticity, community, experiencing a real encounter with a living God, and a greater level of interaction and participation from those that would attend. To create this atmosphere of worship and expectation we utilized candles, incense, and visuals. We wanted to encourage the arts, and provide a place where artists could display their artwork. The time for praise and worship was focused on using songs that would foster that atmosphere of authenticity, intimacy, and a greater sense of participation.

To connect with our culture we use songs that sound like songs that would be heard on the radio. This doesn't necessarily mean heavy electric guitars and loud songs. In fact, often hymns are used, either in their original arrangement or in a modern style. I really believe that, when it comes to this whole praise and worship area and trying to have it connect with people today, it is not so much a *style* issue as it is an *authenticity* issue. People today are starving for something real. We know the most real thing that has ever been or will ever

be is Jesus Christ. So, it's not an issue of "if we should play guitar or keyboard, or if we should use traditional hymns or modern
praise choruses." It's an issue of "can we get out of the way and
let God be the center of the worship?" If we can strip away ourselves enough to show Christ for who he is, people will recognize
him and be drawn to him.

We looked for more and more ways to involve the participants in worship. Communion was an area that lent itself to
emphasizing participation, community, and an authentic
encounter with God. To enhance these aspects of communion we
chose to use communion stations. These stations were small
tables set about the auditorium with the bread and the cup. Each
Sunday communion is a central time of taking together the body
and blood of our Savior as a community of believers. The added
emphasis of getting up out of your seat and walking to a table to
partake, while seeing those that are entering into that same act
with you is powerful. There is a thick sense of community and
interaction that happens every week through communion.

Another example of giving the service back to the
participants is through testimonies. There is
nothing more powerful than hearing real people share real stories
of what God has done and is doing in their lives. We constantly
want to allow people to share how God is working in the community of believers. This shows a transparency and a realness
that resonates with people. They see someone up there talking
who is really no different than they are, and they can relate with
that person. This allows the service to be *their* service and to feel
a little more real.

The message is another area we have used to facilitate
interaction. Following some messages we open it up for a time of
questions and answers. The speaker fields questions from the
audience that deal with the topic just discussed. Although poten-
tially frightening for the one trying to answer the questions, this
has opened up the service and allowed the participants to test
the authenticity of the speakers and removed barriers between
the audience and the teachers. They no longer come to hear
someone preach or lecture on a topic and leave with a "case

closed" feeling. An atmosphere that encourages questioning and deeper understanding is created. This shows that we are not claiming to know it all, but at the same time we are not wandering in the dark either. We are extending the Truth, and the Answer, without pretending to have solved all of life's mysteries.

Periodically we will try to heighten the level of participation even more through different elements or worship stations. This has included everything from people lighting candles to the reinstating of the Old Testament incense offerings as our prayers rise to God. Our assembly has visually incorporated someone worshiping on stage through molding pottery on a wheel or painting a canvas while we display verses about the Master Artist and Painter.

Through the whole process we have seen how God has planted the seed of this service through where we've been. We've watched as that seed grew into an actual living, functioning body of Christ. We have seen it change and grow, with the seasons and with time. And we look forward to the future and to the continuing changes and growth that will occur. Most of all we celebrate the fruit that has been created through this new service. That fruit may be a young artist who is getting to use her gifts and talents for the first time in church. Or it might be someone connecting with and accepting Christ as his or her Lord and Savior for the very first time. Or it might be through hundreds of people, young and old, connecting with each other and with Christ in a life-changing way that may never have happened without the 608 service.

Stories of Swimming Techniques-Within the Community Pool 12

STORY THREE—APEX

A Church-within-a-Church
Las Vegas, Nevada
Joe Boyd, Teaching Pastor

A child forms his or her major personality traits before the age of three. Therefore, if nothing else, allow me to share with you the emerging personality of an active and growing toddler called Apex Church in Las Vegas, Nevada.

Apex was born from the dream of a small group of Bible college students bent on "fixing the problems" of the churches of their youth. Needless to say, for Apex Church to ever be healthy, these seminarians had to eventually see that not all of their motives in church planting were totally pure. However, as is often the case, youthful passion and energy can sometimes buy the time needed to grow into an appropriate measure of humility and grace.

180

Risking Partnership

Early on, only two things were certain: 1) The young church planters were going to need a great measure of help, patience, and resources to chase their dream; and 2) it would take a unique church to partner with the idea of planting a church with a twenty-three-year-old pastor and an unproven philosophy.

Both issues were answered in 1996 when Canyon Ridge Christian Church agreed to support the endeavor. At that time Canyon Ridge itself was only a three-year-old church plant of Central Christian Church in Las Vegas. It had grown tremendously from a core group of around 300 people to nearly 1,500 people in just a few years. The elders of Canyon Ridge saw this new style of church planting as a way to continue the amazing revival that God was starting in "Sin City."

I was brought on staff at Canyon Ridge and given a little over one year to lay the foundation of what would eventually become Apex Church. The partnership was solidified when Kevin Odor became the Senior Pastor of Canyon Ridge in that same year. Kevin was my youth pastor and mentor as a teenager. Our mutual respect and trust has proven to be, apart from the grace of God, the key to the relationship between Canyon Ridge and Apex.

To date, the two churches have shared resources and a common goal to reach the whole person with the whole gospel in Las Vegas. We are still working out the terminology of what we normally simply call "the great experiment." We sometimes refer to Apex as a "church within a church." Sometimes we say that we are "two churches living in community." While other times we truly function as one church. We like to think that the chaos and fluidity gives God the room to do what he wants. So far, we have seen that he is using us to model intergenerational unity and togetherness. Only time will tell how the covenant between Apex and Canyon Ridge will grow and develop. We pray every day for the humility and patience to continue to trust God with this great experiment.

The Early Days

The formation of the Apex Community began in a small group of twelve young adults from Canyon Ridge Church. For nearly fourteen months, this core group met together to lay the foundation of the new church. By September 1997 the core group had grown from just a few to over fifty people who were committed to starting a church that would reach their lost friends with the gospel of Christ.

Apex met as a church body for the first time on September 28, 1997 in the cafeteria of a middle school in northwest Las Vegas. Months of planning had gone into that first church service. The energy was incredible. Dozens of people came early to convert the cafeteria into a place of worship. The worship band had practiced for weeks to pull off two cover songs and a worship set. My sermon had been written and rewritten countless times in the months leading up to the inaugural service. We were ready—almost too ready.

We had been praying for two hundred people to attend the first service, and we had just barely missed our goal. Over one hundred and ninety friends and well wishers came with the excitement that can only accompany the birth of a brand new church. More than twenty people stayed to load the sound equipment back into the old Ryder truck that we shared with Canyon Ridge, still a portable church herself. Though little was said that night, the expressions on the faces of the people spoke volumes: "The dream was a reality; nothing could stop us now!"

"We'll get two hundred people next week," I said with a naïve confidence as I closed the door of Lied Middle School behind me. We didn't. Nor did we the next week, or the next. Actually, we didn't see two hundred people at a worship event for the next forty-seven weeks. We didn't grow. We actually lost about twenty people each week for the rest of the year, until we had "grown" our church from 193 people to an anemic gathering of less than sixty souls in just three months—not exactly the kind of growth that spawns great books!

That infamous week was our emotional and spiritual basement. We couldn't get much lower. We had managed to lose virtually every person except the fifty who started the church, and by this time most of them were burning out and fighting amongst themselves. Something had to give. I drove home alone that December evening, with tears in my eyes. I punched the steering wheel of my car and cursed God for forsaking me. Why would he let *me* fail? Why was he so bent on embarrassing *me?* What had *I* done to deserve this? It was that night that I realized how much of "me" was invested into that little church. It was that night that I was forced to make a choice. It was going to be me (my shaky foundation of dreams and insecurities) or it was going to be God. Thankfully for all of us, God stepped in.

I will never forget that first Sunday in January of 1998. Just seven days after my bout with God, I sat on a stool in front of my little congregation. I told them that I was done pretending. "We can't do this anymore," I resigned. Somewhere along the way we had sacrificed the reality of the Kingdom of God for electronic drums that never quite sounded right and Power Point presentations that never quite looked right. We had sold a life of love and grace for a mediocre presentation of an empty gospel. We had traded joy for image, peace for busyness, and the thrill of God's adventure for a twisted mixture of fear and bitterness. We had offered up a sacrifice too great. And the worst part was that every member of the church knew it, even before I did.

Looking back on that seemingly normal Sunday in January, two breakthroughs occurred that dramatically, though slowly at first, changed the direction of the entire ministry. The first was a vow that I made during the introduction of my message that night. I promised on behalf of all the leaders of the church that we would no longer focus on programs and events that separate real people from the love of God in the name of "church." No more all-day band rehearsals that destroy community. No more flashy church services that turn the dramatic reality of the gospel into a theatrical production complete with popcorn and a thirty-two-ounce soda. No more ignoring the poor and hurting among us for the sake of building a church to feed our egos. It was time to covenant into true community. It was time to very literally practice what we had been preaching for the last three months. It was time to quit *doing* church and start *being* the church. From that Sunday until the present, visitors and members alike have used one word to describe Apex Church: real. For better or worse, we are who we are, and whosoever will may come and join our real community of broken people.

It was going to take an entire conversion of heart and mind to truly build a Christian community from a crowd of strangers. We would have to learn that community is truly a mysterious gift of God and nothing that we "build" or "work on." We would have to surrender our individual egos and agendas to self-sacrificial love. We would have to invest the time into learning each other's names and stories, fears and dreams. We had to figure out a way to live life together. And ever so slowly, through time and prayer, we did eventually became a true community of God-followers. From the ashes of our failed attempts to build a church, Christ himself resurrected a Bride for himself in our midst. To this day, he has yet to complete his mysterious and miraculous work of grace in our community.[1]

It was after the church service that same Sunday meeting in January of 1998 that a 29-year-old local businessman named Jim approached me. Jim and his family had been coming to Apex since the first week but remained virtually unnoticed. I knew him by name only. He had been praying for the church and for me since the first week. His question that night cut to my heart. "Is there a group of people who pray for you?" he asked. My instinctual thought was, "Prayer? We don't have time for that yet. Maybe someday, but we are trying to start a church here." My simple response was, "No, not really."

After a few minutes of conversation, I asked Jim if he would be willing to start a group to pray for the church. He rather sheepishly agreed. After seeing that Jim wasn't very interested in a leadership position in the church, I did what any sensitive pastor would do. I invited this man, whom I really did not know at all, to join three other key leaders and me on a planning retreat regarding the future of the church. (This group would later become the elders of Apex.) In just a few days we were going out of town to try to figure out a way to "save" the church. Jim agreed to at least pray about coming with us. And, thank God, he joined us that weekend in January.

That very week, the five of us locked ourselves in a motel room about forty-five miles west of Las Vegas. I came up with an agenda for our two days together. I had taken the time to sketch out about five different action plans or scenarios to "pull Apex out of its slump." Once we were situated in the room, I passed out my agenda and began to lead a discussion. Jim interrupted, "Shouldn't we pray first?" I could see the other leaders looking at me. I knew exactly what they were thinking, "Who invited the religious guy to the church board meeting?"

But we prayed. For Jim's sake at first, but eventually for our sake, our church's sake, and ultimately for the sake of the gospel. As a matter of fact, we didn't stop praying for two days. We confessed sin. We pleaded with God to save our church. We prayed for church members by name. Jim even received a "vision" of what our church could be someday by God's grace. More amazing than that, the rest of us actually believed him. Needless to say, we emerged from that meeting with one simple action plan: keep *praying* and *be* the church.

Fulfilling the Dream

After three months of leading a church without God's help, we ran into his arms and pleaded for his help. And, to his glory, he has proven faithful ever since. (We had to find out later that sometimes it is even more tempting to leave God out of a church when it is growing and "successful.") Our only truly good days as a church have been when we pray. Unfortunately for us, that is a lesson that we have been forced to learn more than a few times on our journey together.

The dream of Apex was always about reaching those who were far from God with the life-changing, revolutionary love of Christ. It had always been about living the Kingdom of God with the least of these. At its core, Apex was birthed to save the lost and to be salt and light in a city built on illusion and sin. That never changed. And it never will. Apex will always be a church for those who are far from God.

What has changed is the way we reach lost people. Early on, it was very important for our church services to be "excellent" or "cool" or "cutting edge." We spent more time in the culture than in the gospel. We avoided the countercultural parts of Jesus, the mystery of the Trinity, the confusing parts of Paul, and the violent parts of the Old Testament. We accidentally slipped into the business of marketing a politically correct, postmodern, weak-kneed Jesus to a culture just like him. And true seekers didn't want that kind of Jesus. Guess what they yearned for? A countercultural, mysterious, sometimes confusing person who understood life's problems and lived a life consistent to his faith. They wanted Christ, and we were fresh out.

We slowly realized that being sensitive to seekers and postmodern pagans really boiled down to a few simple ideas:

1. Speak into their culture, but be countercultural.

The only subject matter that a Christian should be more familiar with than the pagan culture where he lives is the gospel itself. The timeless and unchanging gospel always falls into an ever-changing culture. Every disciple is called to be a missionary in his or her culture. Every true missionary is called to advance the mission of Christ into a particular group of people. Missionaries must learn the language, music, literature, economy, and pagan religions of a culture to best reach the people. He or she must speak the truth of Christ in a common tongue. The same is true for all churches and missionaries serious about reaching the post-Christian western world.[2] I wake up every morning sure of the fact that I am a missionary to the lost and hurting people of Las Vegas, Nevada, in the year A.D. 2001.

However, we do not preach culture, we preach Christ. Culture is the language; Christ is the Truth. Christ's Kingdom on earth is countercultural. This is, after all, the major thesis of Christ's three-year message as recorded in Matthew 4:17: "From that time on Jesus began to preach, 'Repent, for the kingdom of the heavens is near.'"

2. Be completely open. Don't hold back anything from them.

The tendency in modern evangelism is to "soft sell" Christianity. First, we "hook" a seeker by entertaining them or by touching a felt need. Second, we present a gospel of "sin management"[3] that offers forgiveness of sin and eternal life through the grace of Christ. Usually this step culminates in some sort of simple prayer or perhaps in the sacrament of baptism. After they "believe" we begin "discipleship" through a series of specific programs or classes that direct individuals down a mostly predetermined path of transformation. We save the mysteries and theological biggies for after conversion: worship, communion, giving, service, fasting, celibacy, eschatology, pneumatology, missiology, and all of the other big words.

Postmoderns don't want to be eased into faith. They want to be surrounded by it. They want to see the guts of the whole operation. They don't want to be ushered from the baptistery to the secret room where all the mysteries and theological debates are stored. The want to go through that room on the way to the baptistery. They want to "taste" Christ in the bread and wine. They want to witness authentic worship. They want the Bible to be, at times, complicated and paradoxical; after all, every other worthwhile truth in the world is. It is my opinion that all of the buzzwords surrounding postmodern ministry (think "authentic," "experiential," "participatory") are rooted in this basic idea of not withholding any of the truths or practices of our faith. In his day, Jesus certainly blurred the line between conversion and discipleship, making them interconnected. Perhaps it is time for the church to de-program and teach future converts that true conversion is a discipleship covenant with Christ in the context of the here-and-now Kingdom of Heaven on earth.

3. Be consistent in practice and philosophy.

Perhaps this truth is so obvious that it need not be stated. Postmoderns are always asking if the person pushing the product actually uses it. (Take note of the gradual decline in famous product endorsers and the gradual increase of "normal" people, or at least actors pretending to be normal people.) Similarly, they want to know if those preaching Christ are actually *living* Christ. They want to know if they doubt, if they sin, if they hurt. I have personally operated on what I normally call a 95% belief in God for most of my Christian life. I used to be ashamed of my last 5% full of questions, fears, and doubts. I used to pretend that I had no doubts or questions; after all, I reasoned, I was the preacher! Who wants a preacher who sometimes doubts his own faith? Believe it or not, that question is not rhetorical. Who wants a fallen, confused, hurting, sinning spiritual sage? Postmoderns do. They want to know that their leaders are swimming in the same cesspool of depravity as they are. They want to watch those ahead of them progress and become more like Christ, and if those ahead of them are not honest about their spiritual condition, masking a holy and counterfeit perfection, then there is no journey to watch. I am not saying to use the pulpit as a confessional booth, but there are some sins and struggles that should be shared with the church if they are to follow a flesh and blood leader. The days of following the "perfect example" are gone, or at least they only exist in certain inwardly focused Christian subcultures, not on the front lines of evangelism.

In our context, the rapid "addition" growth of Apex over the last two years (nearly 1,000% growth since our lowest mark) has brought with it many challenges, not the least of which was an unspoken level of contentment about being a "growing" church. As we grew, excitement and energy increased, but once again, the value of community began to decrease. Ironically, the major understanding that "saved" us was accidentally discarded when we began to see our church as a "success." On a practical front, it became impossible to truly be a genuine community of 200, 300, or 500 people. We were too big to live in community. Some people started to long for the "good old days" when everyone knew the name and story of the person sitting beside him at church.

Once again, something had to change. This time, however, the change was needed to somehow maintain the growth of our church. For years, we had flirted with small group ministries, lay-shepherding systems, and involvement programs. We had slipped into a dangerous pattern of reinventing these programs every six months. It seemed that no matter what we would do, the same fifty people would be fully involved (usually to the point of exhaustion), while the others would remain perfectly content to simply attend "church" and go home.

The problem was an educational one. Our people thought that church was something to "attend." It isn't. Church is something you are, or it is nothing at all. Remember why Jesus came? To launch and lead—a Kingdom. Not a meeting. Not a service. Not a program. Not a system. A *Kingdom*. A living, breathing community of King-followers. The disciple of Jesus doesn't "go" to church. He never "leaves" church. He is never "late" for church. He cannot "skip" church or forget church. He *is* the church. That's what *is* is. Twenty-four/seven. Three hundred and sixty-five days a year.

This understanding completely transformed the way we viewed Apex. We were well on the way to developing an elaborate system of holy busyness. The Kingdom was compartmentalized into dozens of lifeless bite-size morsels of worship, teaching, community, and service. Need friends? Join a small group. Need worship? Attend a midweek singing service. Need to serve? Join a ministry team. Need accountability? Start a same-sex accountability group. Need Bible knowledge? Sign up for the next Minor Prophets class. Need to help the poor? Help plan the mission trip. Need to pray? Join the prayer ministry. Need Jesus? Sorry, we're too tired.

Please understand that all of these things are good. Small groups, Bible classes, mission trips and prayer groups have tremendously influenced my own spiritual journey. The problem lies in the practicality that I simply cannot keep up the pace. I need to pray, serve, worship, care, and evangelize every day. I also need to love my family and sleep once in a while, too. How do I do it all? By slowing down. By choosing a simpler path to God.

Ten Distinctives of the House Church

Apex is now a "community of communities" or a "church

of churches." Every member of Apex is now also a member of a "house church,"[4] his or her primary community of faith. House churches are holistic Christian communities of 20-70 people who live life together. Members of a house church covenant with one another to be the church together. Every Apex house church embodies the following ten distinctives:

1. Mission

"Missional" means being on a mission, or being "missionaries" to a culture. House churches must be missional in context. This means that every community sees their church as alien to the culture in which they reside. Every member of a house church community views his world through the eyes of a missionary who exists to be Christ's representative in the culture where he lives. Communities learn to be countercultural in belief and practice while fully understanding the secular culture of their neighborhood or subculture. House churches intentionally interact with lost and hurting people so that they will be able to share the gospel of Christ in word and deed, and incarnate his love through the love of the community.

2. Community

Any person is welcome to attend a house church meeting, but many will choose to do more than simply attend. People who choose to commit to a house church as their primary Christian community will become members of the house church. They enter a community covenant relationship with the other members of the church. They hold their possessions loosely, and are ready to share with anyone who has need. They vow to meet each other's physical, emotional, and spiritual needs so long as God provides and strengthens. Some house churches or smaller groups within churches may voluntarily choose to live communally, literally sharing their lives together on a daily basis.

3. Prayer

Healthy churches pray. Corporate prayer is a part of every house church meeting. House church members pray daily for the lost and for the needs of their community. The sick, afflicted, and troubled are bathed in prayer. The members of the community teach and practice the spiritual disciplines of meditation, fasting, silence, intercession, and solitude.

4. Study

The Bible is elevated within house churches as the inspired and preserved record of God's Word. It is read corporately and individually. House church meetings contain Bible teaching from a member with the teaching gift. The members of the community teach and practice the spiritual disciplines of Bible study, Scripture meditation and memorization. Extrabiblical study of other Christian thinkers is also encouraged.

5. Worship

Every word and action is ultimately seen as worship to God. Worship is taught and practiced as a life of relentless love towards God and mankind. Corporate worship is a part of most meetings, which may or may not include singing, prayer, artistic expression, spirit-led expression, and a myriad of other worship experiences.

6. Accountability

Members of a house church submit to accountability within their community. This includes accountability in regard to both personal sin and personal spiritual growth. Members are weekly asked to share their successes and failures. Sins are confessed and forgiven. Successes are acknowledged and celebrated. It is recommended that accountability meetings take place away from the primary meeting, in same-sex groups of two to five people.

7. Service

A "glocal" worldview is one that sees the world and the church as both local and global at the same time. House churches actively come to the aid of those who are being treated unjustly, both near and far. They feed and clothe the poor, care for widows and orphans, visit prisoners, and pray for the persecuted church.

8. Sacraments

House churches administer the two biblical sacraments instituted by Christ: baptism and communion. Baptisms occur spontaneously within communities as people come to faith in Christ. Communion is offered regularly as a memorial to Christ's death on the cross. When offered, it becomes the centerpiece of the church meeting.

9. Gift-Driven

House churches are structured according to the God-given spiritual gifts of the members. A leadership team of three to eight people is appointed by the Apex elder team to lead every community. These leaders exist to help the members discover and use their spiritual gifts within the community. Whenever possible, every member of a house church is both a mentor and an apprentice to someone who has similar gifts as her own.

10. Church Planting

Every house church is expected to start (plant) a new house church no later than two years from its inception. This is the most organic way to grow the church in any city or culture. Many different methods may be used to plant a house church. All church plants are done with the help and accountability of the Apex elders.

And so that is our story. We are simply a collection of movements: from a gathering of strangers to a small church. From a small church to a larger church. From a larger church to a collection of small churches. I would not trade our story for anything. I love to tell the story of Apex because it is God's story. Jesus said that the Spirit-wind blows where he chooses to blow. He has, thank God, chosen to blow on us. We continue to pray, but these days we are praying more and more for the holy chaos of revival. We pray that God would use us to spark a movement of little churches that work through our depraved city like living yeast through dough. We pray for a day when we lose count. We pray for a day when we lose control and watch God do immeasurably more than we can ask or even imagine. And we never stop praying that his Kingdom come, his will be done, on earth as it is in heaven.

"He who hath not the Church for his Mother, hath not God for his Father."

–Cyprian, AD 250

"To be loved by God means to love God and one's neighbor: community with God becomes community with one another. Expecting the kingdom shapes life and service in the church and unites the believers in one common will. True community and common dedication are the positive results of opposing the present age."[5]

–Eberhard Arnold, 1926

"Christians in a post-modern world will succeed, not by watering down the faith, but by being a counter cultural community that invites people to be shaped by the story of Israel and Jesus."[6]

–Robert Webber, 1999

"A new command I give you: Love one another. As I have loved you, so you must love one another. By this all men will know that you are my disciples, if you love one another."[7]

–Jesus Christ

STORY FOUR—COMMON GROUND
A Church-within-a-Church Plant
Common Ground Christian Church, Indianapolis, Indiana
Jeff Krajewski, Preaching Pastor

My journey began in 1994 when I left Bible college in search of a job. In my beginning stages, I was certain beyond a shadow of a doubt that preaching in a church was not something that I wanted to be involved in. To my delight and dismay, God had other plans. Our journey as a church began in 1995 when six people came together to study God's Word and find its applica-

tion in our lives. We were certainly an eclectic bunch of trans-
plants. Two of us were from Ohio, one from Iowa, one from Los
Angeles, and my wife and I from Kentucky and Indiana respec-
tively. We had all been raised in good, stable church-going homes
and knew that the church was the place for us. Our belief wasn't
born out of a dying love for the body of Christ expressed as a
"church" but because we all knew it was the right thing to do. We
believed that the church and the Bible were the essential tools in
discovering and realizing a relationship with God, but we also
were burdened by the reality that most people our age (20s and
30s) did not embrace that same philosophy.

Our purpose in starting the Bible study was twofold. The
first was selfish to an extent in that we all were looking to develop friendships in our new homes. We gathered at first to fulfill
that need within each of us. The second purpose began to take
shape as we collectively felt the need to somehow provide an
atmosphere of nurture and teaching for those people we were
meeting in our everyday lives who didn't have a relationship with
Jesus. We weren't sure where to go with our second desire, and
so as a group we decided that we would pray about and seek
opportunities to invite people to our study. What happened next
was amazing. People accepted our invitations.

Now, to be honest, we were really only reaching out to people who were just like us. People who were new to the city and
looking for a fellowship that was grounded in the person of Jesus
and Scripture. It aggravated me at first. Person after person
would walk in the door with his Bibles and Christianity and for
a while I thought maybe we were doing something wrong. My
passion was for the nonchurched, the unconnected people.
Where were all the pagans, the people who needed saving? Those
were the people I wanted to reach, but they were nowhere to be
found among our holy and righteous group. Somehow, our fellowship continued to grow. Week after week, more and more people would find their way into the apartment where we met to
study the Bible. One day we found that one of our attendees
played the guitar, and so we added some singing before the study.
We would sing, eat, study, pray, and have an all around good
time. In fact, looking back on the whole evolution of things, if I

could go back to those days, I would. It would certainly be self-ish to retreat to those times, but it was also a sweet time of community building that cannot be had with a large group.

The study grew in number and in depth, and we moved to an apartment clubhouse where we stayed and grew some more. All of this happened while we were a part of the larger Traders Point Christian Church family. I was on staff at the church, in charge of "singles" ministry. We continued to grow, and we decided to move the operation back to church and give it a bit more formality and direction. We started AXIS, our official ministry for Young Adults (incidentally, our AXIS was created before Willow Creek, but I have decided not to pursue any legal action against them). We had a worship band, teaching, small group discussion, food, and twenty-five people our first night. Over the next nine months, we grew to a number around 120. We were outgrowing our space and also losing the relational intimacy that we had valued. It was again time for a change, so we decided that we would expand our ministry around our two strengths: dynamic, corporate worship and Bible teaching.

In our change, we didn't want to lose the mission to connect people in a relationship with Jesus and a relationship with a Christian community. We decided to expand our "structure" (much to my chagrin). We would gather on Saturday night for worship and then throughout the week we would gather in people's homes for a more intimate time of study, worship, and teaching, the idea being that the church would gather for corporate worship and scatter to participate in the reality of the church. Our church would express itself in small-group, home fellowships called "growth groups" (which we stole from a similar congregation in Bloomington, Illinois). In these groups we would include all of the traditional "ministries" that many churches have as a part of their corporate life. Our groups would be encouraged to serve one another in the group as well as others in our city. They would be encouraged to participate in ministry through their growth group. We didn't want the ministry of Common Ground to be a building-focused ministry where teams and committees convened to make decisions and carry out ministry, and we didn't want to require someone to be an official member of our church in order to express her gifts and abilities in service.

Because those groups would be the primary focus for all people who wanted to participate in our church, we adopted a "birthing" strategy for the groups. Instead of starting new groups out of nothing, we birthed new groups out of existing groups. This ensured consistency of vision and direction in new groups and also gave us a pool of people to draw from for leadership development.

During the growth of Common Ground, we were always a subministry of Traders Point Christian Church. We were always connected to the mother congregation and identified ourselves as members of Traders Point. We just attended the Saturday night worship service. In the beginning, Common Ground's audience was primarily single men and women between the ages of 18 and 35. As we continued to grow and change, we found that the style of ministry that we were adopting also resonated with individuals and families outside of our target. We found that our style was less about an age group and more about an attitude.

In 1999, our senior minister and I were having a conversation about the future of Common Ground. We had been witnessing a growing trend within our congregation. There were many people who were attending Common Ground, participating in a Growth Group, placing membership in our church, and they had never been to a Sunday morning service. Howard (Senior Minister) didn't see this as a bad thing, but recognized the possible conflicts of two separate congregations, sharing the same home, with different passions for ministry. We began to pray about what should (if anything) happen next. Out of those prayers and many conversations came the decision to move Common Ground off-site to a new home in a part of our city that was in need of a church.

One night, the Common Ground leadership team gathered to discuss and pray about where God might be leading us. No one had any strong feelings about any particular location and we didn't want to get caught up in the business of land prospecting and acquisition. Our prayer was simple: "God, show us where you want us to go. Make it obvious. We don't want our own desires to get in the way, so send us a clear, unavoidable sign. For instance, a free building would be great." The prayer sounded a bit selfish at the time, but we prayed it with all of our hearts. Two weeks later we received a contact from a Baptist church in the arts community of our city. They were an older congregation who had a very small membership that too was older. The church hadn't been growing for years despite their desire to see people come to know Jesus. They had decided that they were going to close the doors and cease to exist as a church. They had begun praying about an opportunity to **give** their building to a younger congregation who could pick up where they had left off. They didn't want to sell it to just anyone, they wanted to give it away. You can probably see where this is going.

We took possession of this gift in the fall of 2000 and began renovating and updating it. Our hope is to be in our new home no later than May of 2001. As we look back on our journey, it is obvious that God has been directing and leading us for the past five years. As we look forward in our journey we have no doubt that this new challenge will be an opportunity for him to grow us up individually and as a community focused on his mission in the world.

STORY FIVE—EMERGING LEADERSHIP INITIATIVE
Gateway Community Church
Austin, Texas
Ted Beasley, Cofounder of E.L.I. and Pastor

I have thumbed through countless Christian books about my generation, books that painted a dismal picture of the church if it refused to address the issues of postmodernism. The authors take on the role of Old Testament prophets, trying to scream loud enough to awaken a church that has slumbered through the changing of millennia. Such writings tend to be heavy on analysis and light on practical answers. As someone who cares deeply about reaching my generation for Christ, I am left wondering, "What can I do to re-present the church to a lost generation?

Enough already with all of the statistics and doom-saying and anti-Baby Boomer rhetoric, just tell me what I need to do!"

oung leaders who are called by God to share Christ with this postmodern generation are left with two choices: 1) revitalize the existing church, or 2) plant new churches to target unreached pockets of our culture. The trend throughout the nineties was to start subministries within existing churches that were focused on Generation X. The established church would allow their "youth" or "singles" to hold court in the church gym on Saturday nights. These ministries attracted young twenty-somethings into the doors of the church with alternative music, video clips, and a speaker who wore jeans. The common reaction of these "Church-within-a-Church" leaders once they got their ministries off the ground was generally, "Now what?" The church continued, in most cases, to view them as a singles group, not the future leadership of the church. Furthermore, ties to the existing, older church usually meant ties to that church's facility, bureaucracy, and reputation in the community. Despite these frustrations, many who have devoted themselves to the church-within-a-church model have impacted their communities. For that reason, many emerging leaders in our generation will continue this method of pouring new wine into the old skins.

The church planting road seems less appealing to young leaders. Denominations all around the U.S. have ramped up major efforts to see new churches planted, yet the primary problem they have encountered is the absence of a new crop of point leaders. Why are church planters in our generation not emerging? We can identify four reasons:

1. **Lack of vision**. The church lacks passionate, God honoring leaders who are captivated by the challenge of reaching our generation through the local church. Our best leaders are going into the business world to start dot.coms rather than muscling their leadership potential to make Christ's church more effective. Someone needs to light a vision bonfire for our young leaders.

2. **Lack of resources**. If a young leader does venture out to

start an innovative church, he or she has difficulty raising the support to make an extended run at the effort.

3. **Lack of camaraderie**. Businesses that start in partnership are four times more likely to succeed than those that launch with one individual. Few new churches start with a team, which greatly decreases the odds of success. Leaders need a supportive network of other church planters to be effective over the long haul.

4. **Lack of community support**. This is the big one! Emerging leaders generally receive criticism and rebuke about their pioneering approach rather than emotional and relational support from other Christians. In addition, they normally have little or no tie to the power structure of the community in which they are planting, making it difficult to access desirable facilities, obtain permits, or find favor in the established community.

The Emerging Leadership Initiative (E.L.I.) was founded in 1997 with the mission "To mobilize and equip an expanding network of young leaders who will start and multiply evangelistically passionate churches to reach postmoderns for Christ." A national board of business leaders and Gen X pastors came together to propose a plan for removing many of the burdens and barriers to seeing young men and women pursue their dreams of planting prevailing churches for their generation. The group researched the latest trends in church planting and ministry to postmoderns and created a simple, repeatable path for inexperienced young people to receive the vision, resources, team, and support to plant a growing network of like-minded churches. E.L.I. functions in five developmental stages in moving the leader from the vision stage all the way through the launch of a church.

Envision

The first stage of development happens as an emerging leader catches a vision for starting a new church. E.L.I. fans out across the country to college campuses, parachurch organizations, and existing churches to encourage potential church planters out of the shadows. Most people who sense a calling to ministry believe that the only track is through Bible college or seminary. The vision of young leaders ignites when they learn of an aggressive training program that prepares them for the specific challenges of initiating a church for their generation.

Examine

In the next stage applicants are screened for the E.L.I. program. It is critical that potential leaders are carefully examined for the gift of leadership and a history of that leadership demonstrated. Many churches fail due to a lack of leadership in the point person. It is essential that the point person have an entrepreneurial spirit, spiritual maturity, proven character, psychological stability, and communication skills. E.L.I. provides an intensive interviewing process to ensure that only those called and gifted ride point for a team. Typically, screening is done over a period of days and conducted by experienced church planters.

Equip

Historically, the church has trained pastors in theology, yet rarely spends time on leadership training or in-depth spiritual formation. E.L.I. provides training systems for a one to two-year, on-the-job residency in an existing church with a successful track record of reaching postmodern non-Christians. The emerging leader chooses a training church to go study at and receive instruction in three areas: theological education, practical leadership skills, and spiritual formation. Functionally, it is an internship. The intern raises his or her own salary for his or her stint at the training church. He will then work on the staff of the church, helping start new initiatives of evangelism, small groups, assimilation of seekers—aimed to develop the leadership and communication skills necessary to plant a church. Interns interface with multiple lead pastors and experts to help them learn about church in a postmodern context as they work through a curriculum of leadership development. The one-on-one nature of the mentoring by pastors who have planted prepares the intern for the pitfalls of the first few years of a new church work. During the internship, the emerging leader also participates in an on-line customized Master of Divinity program from seminaries that have partnered with E.L.I. Once this one- to two-year program is completed, young leaders are prepared with all of the skills and knowledge they will need to get a postmodern church off the ground.

Empower

Certainly there are many seminary and mentoring programs that prepare leaders for Christian service. E.L.I.'s unique contribution is the establishment of a nationwide network of business partners. Emerging leaders choose a city or area to target for a new church, and E.L.I. links them to business partners in that community. The business partnership consists of ten to fifteen community leaders who have caught the vision of reaching the next generation and desire to see a next-generation church started and multiplied in their community. The business partnership in conjunction with the training church contributions provide the funding to launch the new church. Not only does E.L.I. aid in the funding of the church, it also helps in the networking process for a core team of people in that particular city to work alongside the young church planter.

Expand

The last stage of E.L.I. development is to create an expanding network of training churches. Coded into the DNA of every new church plant is the ability to multiply every two to three years. Each new church plant is expected to consistently train and send new emerging leaders in the E.L.I. paradigm. E.L.I. will network the church leadership together on-line and via conferences for ongoing peer support and learning.

E.L.I. launched its pilot church in Austin, Texas, in the fall of 1998. Selected to lead the beta test of the model were two emerging leaders from Willow Creek Community Church. Austin was selected because of its reputation for being a hotbed of postmodernism. The city itself is the product of a collision between the high tech industry, the political community, the large university population, an extensive arts and music subculture, and an activist mentality that has spawned several major social movements. More than any other city in the South, Austin fits the bill of the postmodern city—highly spiritual, but unchurched. Ninety-five percent of Baby Busters surveyed in the feasibility study for the plant did not attend church regularly.

True to the E.L.I. model, a network of business partners was established in the city to fund and support the new church work. Over $200,000 in seed money was raised to cover staff and operational expenses. For six months prior to the launch of the church, a core group of like-minded young Austinites was envisioned and formed. These core members would become the backbone of the church once it went public—volunteers, small group leaders, artists, musicians, children's workers, elders, etc. Once the core approached a critical mass of about fifty, an aggressive marketing campaign began to establish name recognition for the new church. A combination of press coverage, radio ads, postcard mailers, and a Web site produced a crowd of 250 curious churchgoers the morning of the official launch. Surveys of those who attended the launch revealed that nearly 70% had never attended a church or had not attended in the past ten years. When asked about religious affiliation, many listed Buddhist, Hindu, and "other." The pilot of the E.L.I. paradigm proved to be successful. Within a year of the launch, over 100 previously unchurched individuals had come to faith in Jesus Christ. Not only had they found community in the church, they had begun to bring their own non-Christian friends to explore Christianity there as well. Today, at the tender age of two and one-half years, the Austin church has grown to a weekly attendance of 400 with 300 in small groups.

The Austin church instantly became a training center for further church plants. E.L.I. identified and screened an emerging leader desiring to launch a postmodern church in St. Louis, Missouri. This intern joined the staff of the Austin church for approximately two years, and received a hands-on education in how to plant a church. While this intern trained in Austin and enrolled in the education partnership with Bethel Seminary, E.L.I. was at work creating key business partner relationships in the St. Louis metro area. The St. Louis church was launched after the two-year internship, and has already begun training yet another emerging leader to plant a third generation church.

E.L.I. continues to hone the process for envisioning, identifying, and empowering young men and women to start postmodern churches around the country. E.L.I. training churches can be found in Austin, Denver, San Diego, Cincinnati, and St. Louis. Some day E.L.I. dreams of having a presence in every major metropolitan area of North America. History is filled with examples of how a few emerging leaders can alter the trajectory of a culture. It happened through the missionary church planting movement of the late 1800s. It happened through the parachurch movement of the 1900s. Perhaps God is raising up a new generation of leaders to fan the flame of spiritual renewal in these postmodern times. Now is the time to move beyond mere social commentary about Generation X or postmodernity. Now is the moment for emerging leaders to step forward to take on the challenge of touching a thoroughly secular culture.

─────────────

[1] The following books have been highly instructive in our understanding of biblical community: *Life Together* by Dietrich Bonhoeffer; *Community and Growth* by Jean Vanier; *The Celtic Way of Evangelism* by George Hunter; *Reaching Out* by Henri J.M. Nouwen; and the writings of Eberhard Arnold, particularly *God's Revolution* and *The Early Christians in Their Own Words*.

[2] Read the Essay "The Gospel between Church and Culture" by George Hunsburger in the book by the same title for a deeper understanding of missiological issues in postmodernity.

[3] See chapter 2 of *The Divine Conspiracy* by Dallas Willard, HarperCollins, 1998, for an understanding of the dangers of what he calls the gospel of "sin management."

[4] Visit the Apex Web site at www.apexchurch.org. For similar-minded churches visit the "National" section of The Barnabas Project Web site at www.barnabasproject.org.

[5] Eberhard Arnold, *The Early Christians in Their Own Words* (Farmington, PA: Plough Publishing, 1997), p. 9.

[6] Robert Webber, *Ancient-Future Faith* (Grand Rapids: Baker, 1999), p. 7.

[7] John 13:34-35.

Select Bibliography

Books

Arnold, Eberhard. *God's Revolution: The Witness of Eberhard Arnold*. New York: Paulist Press, 1984.

_____. *The Early Christians in Their Own Words*. Ed. by the Hutterian Society of Brothers and John Howard Yoder. Farmington, PA: Plough Publishing, 1997.

Baugh, Ken, and Rich Hurst. *Getting Real*. Colorado Springs: Navpress, 2000.

Bonhoeffer, Dietrich. *Life Together*. Trans. by John W. Doberstein. New York: Harper & Brothers, 1954.

Chesterton, G.K. *Orthodoxy*. New York: Image Books, 1959.

Finzel, Hans. *The Top Ten Mistakes a Leader Makes*. Wheaton: Victor Books, 1994.

Foster, Richard. *Celebration of Discipline: The Path to Spiritual Growth*. San Francisco: HarperCollins Publishers, 1998.

Grenz, Stanley. *A Primer on Postmodernism*. Grand Rapids: Eerdmans, 1996.

Hunsberger, George. *The Gospel between Church and Culture*. Grand Rapids: Eerdmans, 1996.

Hunter, George G., III. *The Celtic Way of Evangelism*. Nashville: Abingdon, 2000.

Larson, Bruce. *No Longer Strangers*. Waco: Word, 1971.

McAllister, Dawson. *Saving the Millennial Generation*. Nashville: Thomas Nelson, 1999.

McIntosh, Gary L. *Three Generations*. Grand Rapids: Revell, 1995.

Nouwen, Henri J.M. *Reaching Out*. Garden City, NY: Image Books, 1986.

Starkey, Mike. *God, Sex & the Search for Lost Wonder*. Downers Grove, IL: InterVarsity, 1997.

Sweet, Leonard. *Aqua Church: Essential Leadership Arts for Piloting Your Church in Today's Fluid Culture*. Loveland, CO: Group Publishing, 1999.

————. *Postmodern Pilgrims*. Nashville: Broadman & Holman, 2000.

Tichey, Noel M. *The Leadership Engine*. New York: Harper Collins, 1997.

Vanier, Jean. *Community and Growth*. 2nd, Revised Ed. New York: Paulist Press, 1989.

Walter, Darren. *The People-Magnet Church*. Joplin, MO: College Press, 2001.

Warren, Rick. *The Purpose-Driven Church*. Grand Rapids: Zondervan, 1995.

Webber, Robert. *Ancient-Future Faith*. Grand Rapids: Baker, 1999.

Willard, Dallas. *The Divine Conspiracy*. Grand Rapids: HarperCollins, 1998.

Yancey, Philip. *Reaching for the Invisible God*. Grand Rapids: Zondervan, 2000.

OTHER RESOURCES

David Aaron Murray, *First Things*. No. 73, May 1997.

Web essay by Mark Driscoll, *Postmodernity*, www.marshill.fm.

Apex Web site at www.apexchurch.org. For similar minded churches visit the "National" section of The Barnabas Project Web site at www.barnabasproject.org.

About the Authors

Jeff Krajewski currently serves with the Common Ground Christian Church in Indianapolis, Indiana. Previously he served as Minister of Young Adults with the Trader's Point Christian Church in Indianapolis.

Jeff graduated from Cincinnati Bible College and Seminary with a Bachelor of Science degree in Christian Ministries. He is maried to Nicole and they have two adorable children, Tucker and Kezley. Jeff loves to spend time with his family and play golf whenever possible.

Rusty George serves the Southland Christian Church in Lexington, Kentucky, working with the weekend postmodern-targeted worship service.

Rusty graduated from Ozark Christian College in Joplin, Missouri, with Bachelor of Theology and Bachelor of Sacred Literature degrees. He is completing his Master's degree in Theology with Cincinnati Bible College and Seminary. Rusty is married to Lorrie and they live in the Lexington area. He is passionate about basketball, not entirely due to his current location.

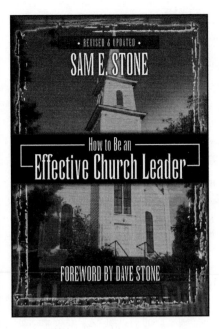

How To Be An Effective Church Leader
Sam Stone

In this book, Sam Stone lays the foundation for effective leadership by combining principles taken straight from Scripture with practical advice from life experience. He reminds us that churches can only do their best work when excellent leadership is present. He tackles timely topics like

- the real head of the church
- qualities of a good leader
- the spiritual disciplines a leader must practice
- the expectations a leader will face
- suggestions for maximizing board meetings
- dynamics of the preacher/elder relationship

If you are considering a church leadership position, or even if you are a veteran leader, Sam Stone's timeless advice will provide you with insight and encouragement.

110 pages, soft, #HC-899-2, $8.99

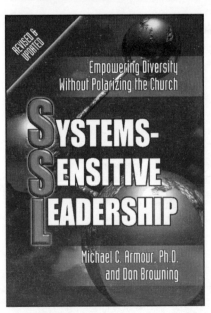

Systems-Sensitive Leadership: Empowering Diversity without Polarizing the Church
Michael C. Armour and Don Browning

God demonstrated his creativity even in our personalities. People view events from different perspectives and presuppositions. Whether it is conflict resolution, goal achievement, or completing a specific task, a systems-sensitive leader will be able to recognize the differences in people and help them to work together toward common objectives. This is a must read book for anyone involved in church or business leadership.

300 pages, soft, #HC-814-3, $14.99

Making Your Church A Place to Serve
Involving Members the Southeast Way
Don Waddell

The statistics are staggering. Thom Rainer in his book *High Expectations* found that if members of a church only attend worship services, only 16% will still be attending in five years. If however they become an active part of a Sunday School, that percentage goes up to 83%.

Southeast Christian Church does not claim to have all the answers, and this is not a magic book of formulas, plans, programs, or gimmicks. Rather it defines a process toward inviting people to an intimate relationship with God. The CD contains 200 pages of letters, phone scripts, bulletin inserts, applications, etc., which are being used in the ministry at Southeast Christian Church. When you purchase the CD, you have permission(see copyright conditions on pages 8 and 44 of the book), to reformat and reprint this material to fit your church needs. This is an excellent resource and will be a great help in the ministry of your church.

160 pages, soft, #HC870, reg. Price $10.99 • CD (appendix), reg. Price $6.99

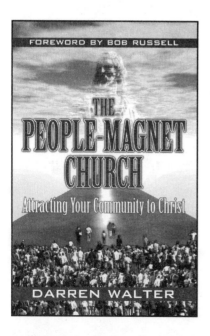

The People-Magnet Church
Darren Walter

Extremely practical and easy to read, Darren Walter offers a multitude of suggestions on making a church a people magnet. Walter calls us to lift up the cross in this lost world and watch as people are drawn to the magnetic love, truth, and grace of Jesus Christ. The message the church carries will forever remain unchanged, while our method in presenting this good news must adapt to fit the current culture. These two combine to form the mission of any church that is committed to becoming a people magnet in its world. By being intentional about the type of church we want to be, we will communicate to the world around us that we are passionate about the God we serve. In turn, God himself will draw people to His church. Becoming a people-magnet church does not sacrifice the integrity of the church or its message, rather it allows us to become more like our Savior who was and is the ultimate people magnet.

150 pages, soft, #HC-872-0, Reg. $11.99